# Government: America's #1 Growth Industry

## How the Relentless Growth of Government is Impoverishing America

by Stephen Moore

Published by
**Institute for Policy Innovation**
250 South Stemmons, Suite 306
Lewisville, TX 75067
(214) 219-0811

**A Word About Sources**

The standard sources used in this book include U.S. Census Bureau, *Historical Statistics of the United States: Colonial Times to 1970*, and *U.S. Statistical Abstract*, various years; Advisory Commission on Intergovernmental Relations, *Significant Features of Fiscal Federalism, 1992*; and Office of Management and Budget, *Budget of the United States Government*, various years, historical tables. Otherwise, sources accompany tables and figures.

Government: America's #1 Growth Industry

All Rights Reserved
Copyright © 1995 Institute for Policy Innovation
Cover design copyright © 1995 Institute for Policy Innovation

No part of this book may be reproduced or transmitted in any form or by any means, electronic or mechanical, including photocopying, recording, or by any information storage and retrieval system, without permission in writing from the publisher, *unless such reproduction is properly attributed, and unless such reproduction is clearly and legibly identified on every page, screen, or field* as "Copyright © 1995 Institute for Policy Innovation."

Printed in the United States of America

Note: Nothing written here should be construed as an attempt to influence the passage of any legislation before Congress. The views expressed in this publication are the opinions of the author, and do not necessarily reflect the views of the Institute for Policy Innovation or those of its directors.

# Contents

Introduction ..................................................... 1

1    2020: A Budget Odyssey ........................... 5

2    Paradise Lost? ............................................ 23

3    Other People's Money ............................... 41

4    Feeding the Beast ...................................... 65

5    The Regulatory Stranglehold ................... 85

6    The Federal Octopus .................................. 95

Conclusion: Taking Back Washington ... 109

# INTRODUCTION

# Government: America's #1 Growth Industry

*On the hope of our free economy rests the hope of all free nations.*
-John F. Kennedy

*"How did an allegedly free people spawn a vast, rampant cuttlefish of dominion with its tentacles in every orifice of the body politic?"*
-P.J. O'Rourke

There is a crisis in America today.

But it is not the kind of crisis that grabs newspaper headlines or lead stories on the evening news. It is not a health care crisis. It is not AIDs or homelessness. It is not an education crisis. It is not the infrastructure. And it is not even the budget deficit. Those are all serious national problems, but none of them is the underlying cancer that is eroding our economic well-being in America today.

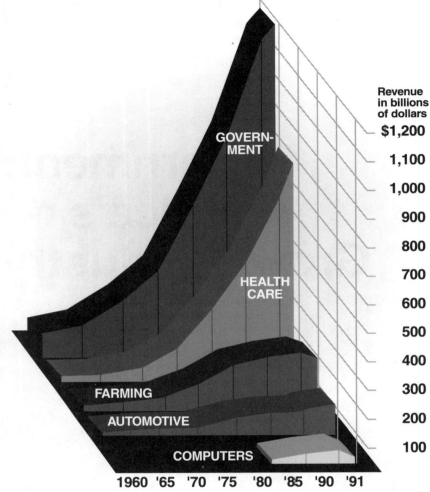

Source: *Reader's Digest*, July 1993, p. 129. Adapted from IPI Policy Report #126, *Government: America's No. 1 Growth Industry.*

America is not confronted with a conventional crisis where we can demand that politicians do *something*—hold congressional hearings, appoint a commission, create new programs, enact new regulations, spend more money, pass more laws.

The crisis in America today simply cannot be solved by new government remedies—no matter how nobly-intended.

Why? Because the crisis *is* government. Government's relentless growth in this century threatens to capsize the 200-year American experiment in freedom and self-government. The rise

## Introduction

of the cradle-to-grave nanny state we have erected in America is not just undermining our economic prosperity—though it is certainly doing that. It is also eroding our basic freedoms and casting away our liberties. The U.S. Constitution that was meant to safeguard those liberties has been largely disregarded by the powers that be in Washington as an outmoded nuisance.

Few Americans fully appreciate how gargantuan our government in Washington has become. Today, government at all levels spends $24,000 for every household in America. Another way to conceptualize the size of our government today is this: With the $2.5 trillion that local, state and federal governments spend each year, you could purchase all the farmland in the United States, plus all the assets of the Fortune 100 companies.

This book documents with charts, tables, statistics, and anecdotes how unrestrained government is making Americans poorer and less free. But this message is summarized concisely in the graphic at left. Our "limited" government is larger than the manufacturing sector, larger than agriculture, the computer industry, and even health care—and it's growing faster than these industries as well. *Sadly, there are more people working for the government than there are working in all our manufacturing industries combined.*

America has fought a Revolutionary War, a Civil War, and two World Wars to protect and preserve our basic liberties and freedoms when they were under assault. Now battles won on foreign fields at the cost of hundreds of thousands of lives are being lost at home. What could be more depressing than to witness Americans *voluntarily* ceding to government the liberties and responsibilities Americans fought and died to protect for the people.

When the American patriot Thomas Paine wrote his 1776 classic *Common Sense*, he repeatedly warned of this very turn of events. He admonished: "Government even in its best state is but a necessary evil," and he went on to argue that when government grows excessive in its powers, "Our calamities will be heightened by reflecting that we furnish the means by which we suffer." In so many ways, those prophetic words have come back to haunt us in modern America.

The questions we need to ask are: How? And why?

And most importantly: What can we do about it?

# 1

# 2020: A Budget Odyssey

*"The natural progress of things is for liberty to yield and government to gain ground."*
-Thomas Jefferson

Imagine the headlines for January 24, 2020:

**PRESIDENT PROPOSES $6 TRILLION BUDGET, RECORD TAX HIKE**

**INTEREST RATES SURGE, DOW PLUMMETS**

Washington, D.C.— The President released his fiscal year 2021 budget blueprint today, a plan which calls for the first $6 trillion budget in U.S. history and a $600 billion tax hike—the largest tax increase in American history. At least $400 billion of these funds are targeted for bailing out the financially insolvent Social Security Administration.

In his budget message the President said that his budget proposal, entitled "Putting America's Fiscal House in Order," will require "shared sacrifice to finally

## 2020: A Budget Odyssey

bring to an end the past three decades of fiscal malpractice in Washington."

"No one likes to pay more taxes, and I don't like having to ask them of you, but every American must participate in this crusade against red ink and runaway spending," the President pleaded. "Without these changes, we face a future of $1 trillion deficits for as far as the eye can see." But the White House conceded that even with these new taxes, the national debt will exceed $16 trillion in 2020 and the deficit will be reduced only to $640 billion.

The majority leader of Congress immediately attacked the concept of raising taxes in a recession. "This is the sixth tax hike in eight years, but the tide of red ink keeps rising," the Nebraska Senator warned. "You can't draw blood from a stone," she said of beleaguered taxpayers.

The President devoted much of his speech to the bail-out of Social Security. "For the past twenty-five years there has been a bipartisan conspiracy in Washington to walk off with retirement money from the federal vault; the day of reckoning is here," he announced. Budget documents reveal that the deficit in the trust fund is expected to climb to a record $400 billion next year—the equivalent of more than $150,000 per retiree. Benefit levels have already been cut by 14 percent over the past three years and the President calls for raising the payroll tax another two percentage points to 24 percent next year.

The President's plan is not all pain and suffering, however. The White House proposes a $450 billion spending increase for what he calls "neglected priorities"—a category which includes education, unemployment insurance, infrastructure, and home building. But a spokesman for the Children's Defense Fund protested that we will never succeed in alleviating poverty, homelessness, and illiteracy if the government is willing to spend only "nickels and dimes."

An ABC/*New York Times* poll taken after the speech indicated that only 18 percent of the public believes the plan will bring down the budget deficit. More than six in ten Americans said they think the deficit will get worse, not better if the plan is adopted. "The public has learned that these budget plans have a perfect record of failure," said a National Taxpayer's Union press release.

A record 91 percent of the public said they now support a constitutional amendment to balance the budget, an idea the President denounced as "fool's gold." What we need from Congress "is courage, not the Constitution, to deal with the evils of big deficits," he insisted. "Trying to bring the deficit down too quickly would be extremely dangerous and economically muddleheaded," added the Chairman of the Council of Economic Advisers.

Financial markets accelerated their year-long tumble and interest rates soared after the President's message. The thirty-year T-bill rate hit a new high of 14.25 percent, and home mortgage interest rates are now over 20 percent. "Despite all the fancy slogans, Washington simply has depleted its last ounce of credibility on the budget deficit," complained the chief economist at Citibank. "The real tragedy is that Congress refused to take action more than twenty years ago to head off this financial train wreck," he added.

In a related story, soon after the President's announcement, a group of more than 8,000 angry demonstrators, almost all under the age of 30, gathered in front of the White House to protest the proposed hike in the Social Security tax. At one point the protesters began chanting: "Hey, hey, we won't pay," as they burned their Social Security cards. When several hundred senior citizens arrived for a counter-demonstration organized by the American Association of Retired Persons, the Capitol police had to be called in to maintain order. "Welcome to the age of generational warfare," said one young woman from Cleveland who helped organize the march on the White House.

Is this news story from the year 2020 an improbable doomsday scenario? Is our government really headed for such a tragic financial train wreck? Are the young and the old going to be pitted against each other in a political battle royal?

Unfortunately, the answer is that something very much like this *could* happen early in the next century, *if* Congress continues to spend and tax and borrow and regulate and mandate over the next thirty years at the same pace that it has over the past forty. That is, if we simply stay on the course we are on, then this doomsday scenario could become a *likely* scenario.

So before we discuss how to avoid this gloomy outlook in the next century, let's first investigate the full implications of the "stay the course" fiscal option. This should underscore why it is essential that, as a nation, we DO change course.

◆ **The Past as Prologue**

Just how much more government can we expect in coming decades?

One useful guide for answering this question is to examine the trends in government spending in recent decades. Federal spending consumed just 16 percent of GDP in 1950, but 24 percent in 1994. In real dollars this was a six-fold increase in the federal budget since 1950; a doubling since 1970; and a 50 percent rise since 1980.

## 2020: A Budget Odyssey

Let's briefly review where all this money has been spent. Table 1-1 shows the patterns of budget growth since 1950. It reveals several important trends:

**An era of near-universal budget expansion** — Over the past four decades almost every major component of the federal budget has increased in real dollars. The two exceptions to the rule are foreign assistance programs and veterans programs. (Veterans benefits were high in the immediate aftermath of World War II but have since declined slightly.)

Table 1-1
Growth in Real Federal Expenditures, 1950-1994 (Billions of $1990)

|  | 1950 | 1960 | 1970 | 1980 | 1994 | Annual Growth 1950-1991 |
|---|---|---|---|---|---|---|
| National Defense | $75.4 | $215.2 | $278.7 | $215.4 | $262 | 2.9% |
| Health | 1.7 | 3.6 | 41.3 | 88.9 | 215 | 11.8% |
| Income Security | 22.6 | 33.1 | 53.2 | 139.1 | 188 | 5.1% |
| Social Security | 4.4 | 51.9 | 103.4 | 190.5 | 275 | 10.1% |
| Education & Social Services | 1.1 | 4.5 | 29.3 | 51.1 | 48 | 9.2% |
| Veterans Benefits | 46.3 | 10.0 | 12.4 | 39.0 | 32 | -0.8% |
| Community Development | 0.6 | 0.9 | 8.2 | 15.1 | 9 | 6.5% |
| Interest | 26.4 | 30.9 | 49.1 | 84.4 | 182 | 4.6% |
| International Affairs | 25.9 | 13.4 | 14.7 | 20.4 | 17 | -1.0% |
| Science & Technology | 0.6 | 2.7 | 15.4 | 9.3 | 15 | 7.8% |
| Agriculture | 11.0 | 11.6 | 17.7 | 14.1 | 20 | 1.4% |
| Justice/General Government | 6.6 | 7.2 | 11.3 | 28.9 | 27 | 3.4% |
| Transportation | 5.5 | 18.3 | 23.9 | 34.2 | 33 | 4.3% |
| Commerce/Housing Credit | 5.5 | 7.1 | 7.2 | 80.0 | 9 | 1.1% |
| Energy/Natural Resources | 8.8 | 9.4 | 14.0 | 38.7 | 25 | 2.4% |
| Offsetting Receipts | 9.9 | 21.5 | 29.3 | 32.0 | 34 | 3.1% |
| Total Spending | $235.0 | $410.0 | $670.0 | $950.0 | $1,324.0 | 4.1% |

Source: *Budget of the United States Government*, Historical Tables, 1994.

**Runaway entitlement spending** — Entitlements are the driving force behind budgetary expansion. *Federal entitlement spending in real dollars has doubled roughly every eight years since 1950.* Outlays for Social Security, health care, and welfare programs are five to ten times larger today in inflation-adjusted dollars than in 1950. To borrow an appropriate analogy from former Office of Management and Budget Director Richard Darman, entitlements are like relentless Pac-Men gobbling up the nation's economic resources.

**Defense budget growing since 1950 but shrinking as a share of GDP** — Defense spending has been growing, though irregularly, since the 1950s. However, as discussed earlier, at less than five percent of GDP, defense spending in 1993 is well below its average in the 1950s and 1960s. Defense spending consumes only about half the share of GDP today than it did in the 1950s and 1960s. Furthermore, defense has been shrinking as a percentage of the federal budget consistently since the 1960s from about 40 percent of the budget to about 20 percent.

**Outlays for federal lending and interest on debt expanding** — Federal credit programs and interest on the national debt are two other fast-growing areas of the budget. As the federal budget deficit continues to grow (it is now $250 billion) interest payments also climb rapidly. Meanwhile, the savings and loan cleanup added an estimated $300 billion to federal outlays. Although this particular crisis is over, at least temporarily, there is now concern that the Federal Deposit Insurance Corporation, the Federal Housing Administration, and the Pension Benefit Guaranty Corporation will soon require multi-billion dollar taxpayer bailouts of their own.

**Domestic discretionary spending slowed in 1980s** — Most domestic discretionary programs — including agriculture, transportation, natural resources, social services, general government, and science — expanded sharply from 1950 to 1980. In the 1980s the Reagan Administration had marginal success in trimming these programs. Their budgets in real dollars (but not in nominal dollars) declined in some cases. Nonetheless, without exception these domestic discretionary programs are considerably larger today than in 1950 and, as discussed in an earlier chapter, they are growing rapidly again so far in the 1990s.

## 2020: A Budget Odyssey

The picture that emerges from this brief review of post-World War II federal fiscal policy is this: Although virtually every area of the budget has expanded sharply since 1950, entitlements are the primary villain in the loss of federal fiscal discipline.

### ◆ A Glimpse into Our Fiscal Future

To project the level and composition of spending over the next three decades, we make four assumptions about the U.S. economy and fiscal priorities:

**ASSUMPTION #1.** Real GDP will grow at a two percent real annual rate over the next thirty years, which is consistent with the predictions of the Social Security Administration.

**ASSUMPTION #2.** Defense spending will average 4.5 percent of GDP—well below its post-World War II average—and remain constant at that level.

**ASSUMPTION #3.** Social Security and health care expenditures will rise at the rate forecasted by the Social Security Administration (assumption 2-B of the 1991 trustees report) and the Health Care Financing Administration. This assumes no new or expanded benefits over the next twenty years.

**ASSUMPTION #4.** Discretionary programs in the budget will grow at their real annual rate of growth from 1950 to 1990. That is, we extrapolate their budget totals over the next 30 years based on their growth over the past 40 years.

The results that emerge from these reasonable assumptions paints a bleak picture of America's fiscal future. Table 1-2 shows the breakdown of spending for major components of the budget.

In the absence of dramatic reform, government expansion relative to the private economy will accelerate at an alarming and economically unsustainable rate:

- The federal government alone will consume 27 percent of GDP by the year 2000, 32 percent of GDP by the year 2010, and 41 percent by the year 2020. See Figure 1-1. Even if state and local spending simply remains constant as a share of the economy, by 2020 more than half of all economic output will be directly controlled by the government.

- In 1990 dollars, the federal budget by the year 2000 will reach $1.8 trillion, by the year 2010 it will exceed $2.5 trillion, and by 2020 the budget will approach $4 trillion.

## 2020: A Budget Odyssey

Table 1-2
Federal Outlays, by function (billions of $1990)

|  | 1993* | 2000** | 2010** | 2020** |
|---|---|---|---|---|
| National Defense | 262.4 | 291 | 359 | 410 |
| Health | 214.6 | 407 | 580 | 760 |
| Income Security | 188.5 | 266 | 436 | 714 |
| Social Security | 275.0 | 310 | 380 | 550 |
| Education and Social Services | 48.2 | 89 | 215 | 517 |
| Veterans Benefits | 32.1 | 30 | 28 | 26 |
| Community Development | 9.0 | 14 | 26 | 49 |
| Interest | 182.1 | 249 | 391 | 613 |
| International Affairs | 16.6 | 15 | 14 | 13 |
| Science, Technology, and Space | 15.4 | 26 | 56 | 118 |
| Agriculture | 19.8 | 22 | 25 | 29 |
| Justice and General Government | 27.4 | 35 | 48 | 67 |
| Transportation | 33.3 | 45 | 68 | 103 |
| Commerce and Housing Credit | 8.7 | 9 | 11 | 12 |
| Energy and Natural Resources | 24.8 | 29 | 37 | 48 |
| Offsetting Receipts | (33.5) | (41) | (54) | (72) |
| Total Spending | 1,324.4 | 1,797 | 2,618 | 3,955 |
| Gross Domestic Product | 5,747.5 | 6,560 | 8,180 | 9,600 |

*Estimates from 1994 budget
**All projections were done using the average annual growth rate for 1950-93, except those for National Defense, Health, Social Security, and Gross Domestic Product, which were done by a different methodology.

Figure 1-1
Federal Spending Will Outpace Economy, 1950-2020

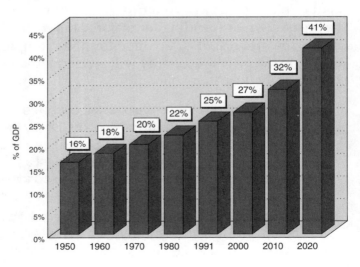

# 2020: A Budget Odyssey

- Total federal liabilities will surpass $20 trillion by the end of the century. This will represent a debt of almost $300,000 for every family of four in the U.S.
- Entitlement spending—health care, Social Security, and income security—will continue to undergo explosive growth. Figure 1-2 shows that outlays will reach nearly $1 trillion (1990 dollars) by the year 2000 and $1.4 trillion in 2010, or just less than is spent on the entire federal budget today. By 2020 entitlements alone will consume the same share of GDP as the entire budget does today.

Figure 1-2
Projected Growth in Entitlements, 1950-2020

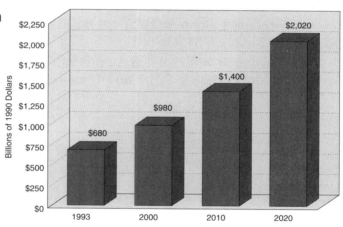

- Real spending on domestic discretionary programs—social services, community development, science and space, and so on—will double in ten years and quadruple in twenty years, as they did in the 1950-1991 period. By 2020 total discretionary domestic programs will consume roughly twice the level of GDP that they do today.
- The fastest growing areas of the domestic, non-entitlement budget will be education and social services spending. These programs will see their budgets rise tenfold in real dollars over the next 30 years—up from $48 billion to $500 billion.

### ◆ Paying the Piper

How will Congress pay for this orgy of new spending? Debt and taxes, of course.

Over the post-World War II period federal taxes have averaged roughly 18.5 percent of GDP. Today taxes consume roughly 19 percent of GDP. Let's assume that federal taxes rise steadily to 25 percent of GDP by the year 2020. This would constitute a federal tax burden much higher than ever before in peacetime. Under this scenario the deficit would still skyrocket to nearly inconceivable levels early next century. Figures 1-3 shows:

- The deficit in 1990 dollars will swell to over $300 billion by 2000, $600 billion in 2010, and $1.4 trillion by 2020.
- The deficit alone in 2020 will be as large as the entire 1992 budget, $1.4 trillion.
- The deficit will reach 5.5 percent of GDP in 2000, 8 percent of GDP in 2010, and 16 percent of GDP in 2020.

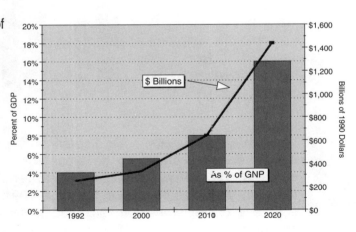

Figure 1-3
Projected Size of the Federal Deficit: Total Dollars and as Share of GDP

If the deficit climbs to these forecasted levels, then clearly interest expenditures—what we pay to finance the national debt—will also skyrocket over the next three decades. Figure 1-4 underscores the magnitude of the crisis:

*2020: A Budget Odyssey*

- Annual interest payments in 1990 dollars will reach $300 billion by 2000 and a staggering $760 billion by 2020.
- Real interest payments will grow by nearly five percent per year for the next thirty years—or two-and-a-half times the expected rate of real economic growth over this period.
- Nearly one of every six dollars that Uncle Sam spends will go toward paying interest on the national debt.

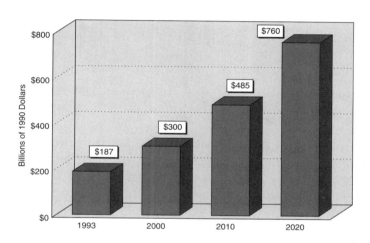

Figure 1-4
Interest on the National Debt, 1993-2020

An alternative to running these massive deficits would be for Congress to attempt to balance the budget by simply raising taxes to match annual spending. As Figure 1-5 shows, this would require tax burdens to rise to almost unthinkable levels:

- On average, by 2020, the average American worker would pay $26,600 (in 1990 dollars) in federal taxes.
- Federal taxes as a share of worker income would have to rise by 20 percent above current levels by 2000; 75 percent above current levels by 2010; and roughly *two-and-a-half-times* the current levels by 2020.
- One-third of all worker income would be taken by the federal government in 2010 and more than 40 percent would be seized in 2020. With state-local taxes, the government's take could rise to 60 percent of middle-income worker paychecks by the third decade of the twenty-first century.

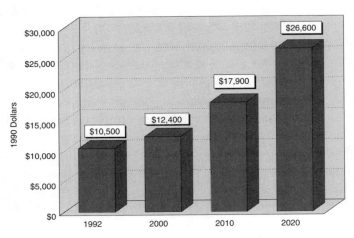

Figure 1-5
Future Federal Taxes per Worker to Balance the Budget

Source: Author's calculations based on Census Bureau data and budgetary predictions

### ◆ Generational Inequity

One way to measure future tax burdens on American citizens is to examine the percentage of lifetime income that future generations of workers will pay in taxes. As Figure 1-6 indicates, as government has grown over this century, this percentage has steadily risen from 24 percent in 1900 to an expected 36 percent for those born in 1990. For children born in the next century, however, the continued expansion of government, *plus* the huge cost of servicing the $5 trillion debt largely built up over the past twenty years mean that this share of lifetime earnings surren-

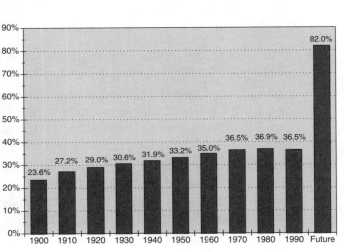

Figure 1-6
Share of Lifetime Income Paid as Taxes

Source: Laurence Kotlikoff and Allen Auerbach, *U.S. Savings Crisis*, prepared for Merrill Lynch, 1994.

dered to taxes is expected to accelerate, reaching as high as 82 percent. Because of the large reliance on borrowing to pay for government, the typical American now pays about 75 cents for every dollar of government benefits received. But in the next century, as this debt gets paid off, Americans could be paying about $1.25 for every dollar of government services received. *If Americans now think that government is a waste of money, just think how our kids, and our kids' kids will feel when nearly one-fourth of their tax dollars go to pay the interest on spending that occurred many years previously.*

### ◆ Social Insecurity

Adding insult to injury for young workers and those who have not yet even entered the workplace are the dire financial straits of Social Security. In early 1994 federal officials conceded that the Social Security Administration will run out of money by 2029—seven years earlier than previously thought. This time bomb will explode right smack in the middle of the retirement years of most baby boomers and well before post-baby boomers are eligible to receive a penny of benefits.

Sadly, even that projection is absurdly optimistic. By 1999 the combined Social Security and Medicare trust funds start spending $8 billion a year more than will be collected in payroll taxes. And that annual deficit will soon thereafter mushroom to more than $100 billion. Since the surpluses of the 1980s and 1990s have already been spent by Congress on everything from maple syrup research to pornographic arts subsidies to nuclear submarines, the program is in much worse shape than anyone in Washington cares to admit.

Few Americans appreciate just how awful an investment Social Security is for those now entering the workforce—the MTV generation. The post-baby boomers will be asked to pay a massive payroll tax burden in exchange for a meager retirement benefit. Here are the grim calculations:

- ◆ A worker just now entering the labor force with an average starting salary of $22,500, and with a normal lifetime earnings path, is expected upon retirement to receive a Social Security benefit of about $12,500 per year (1990 dollars). (This, of course, optimistically assumes that the program is still around in 2040.)

- If that same worker were permitted simply to place his payroll taxes in an annuity with a six percent real rate of return, he would have a nest egg worth almost $800,000 (1990 dollars) at retirement age. This would allow the worker to draw a $60,000 benefit per year until death (assumed at age 80). That's about *five times* higher than what Social Security offers for the same level of investment.

- To state this another way: Workers just now entering the labor market will spend half their working years—that is up until the age of 45—paying Social Security taxes and receiving nothing in return for those contributions. *Assuming a normal rate of return, a worker could start contributing the amount now paid in Social Security taxes into an annuity at the age of 45 and receive the same type of benefit that Social Security offers for paying into the system more than 20 years earlier.*

For today's young workers, then, Social Security isn't generational inequity; it's generational thievery.

### ◆ Is Doomsday Really on the Horizon?

The analysis above shows what might happen if we leave government on automatic pilot. In reviewing the calculations in this chapter, it is tempting to conclude that surely our elected officials could not be that reckless and irresponsible. They must have the foresight and wisdom to realize that if government gets too much larger than it is today, we could be seriously imperiling our children's economic future. And if the current batch of politicians won't recognize this, then surely we the voters will replace them with intelligent people who do.

Yet there are several reasons to suspect that the nation may disregard these caution signs:

**1) Washington's Woeful Recent Fiscal Record.** In the first six post-Reagan years, federal spending, taxes, and regulation have already grown by roughly one-third. Under George Bush and Bill Clinton the pace of federal government spending growth has resumed its 1960s and 1970s pace of expansion. In 1990 and again in 1993 the two largest tax increases in American history were enacted by Congress. Figure 1-7 shows projected spending and debt through 1998 under Clinton.

## Figure 1-7
### Spending and Debt Buildup under Clinton

Source: Congressional Budget Office, *The Economic and Budget Outlook*, August 1994.

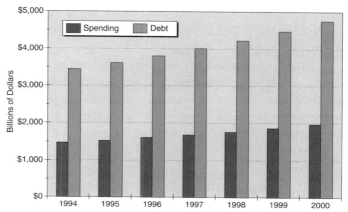

2) **The Demographic Time Bomb.** Without making major changes and fundamentally restructing entitlements, Congress may not be capable of controlling spending. The reason for this pessimism: The aging of the American workforce. Most of our entitlement spending today is directed toward the elderly. The percentage of the population over the age of 65 and eligible for Social Security and Medicare will double by the middle of the twenty-first century. In the year 2020 the number of Americans over 65 will climb to 40 million, up from about 30 million today. In 1970 there were roughly four workers for every retiree. In 1990 this ratio was three workers per retiree. By 2030, when the baby boomers are all retired, there will be only two workers for every Social Security recipient. By that year the feds will owe the baby boomers an estimated $10 trillion in promised Social Security payments, and perhaps as much in health care benefits.

3) **A Government Hostile to Free Enterprise.** A strong argument could be made that the most recent Congress was the most hostile to the free enterprise system that ever assembled in Washington. In 1991 and 1992 Congress proposed $8 of new spending for every $1 of spending reductions. Making matters worse, with Bill Clinton in the White House, no longer do taxpayers have a President willing to serve as a goalie guarding the federal treasury—swatting away new expensive and expansive congressional spending proposals. Nobel prize winning economist Milton Friedman was probably accurate when he recently lamented that

"the Clinton Administration is far and away the most socialist administration in American history." In sum, our most recent cast of characters in Washington had a strong ideological bias toward spending money, not saving it.

**5) A pro-spending bias in the budget process.** Politicians vastly prefer playing Santa Claus to playing Scrooge. Unfortunately, the budget rules reward profligate spending, and discourage responsible restraint. The 1990 budget agreement has proven to be a sensational fraud. Meanwhile Congress continues to ignore public demands for genuine budget forms, such as a balanced budget amendment or a tax/spending limitation requirement.

All of these features of the political environment in Washington point to the same depressing conclusion: As things now stand, America is headed toward a twenty-first century with much more government, not less.

### ◆ The Stages of National Poverty

We do not have to imagine the consequences of allowing government to continue to grow uncontrollably. We know from the lessons of both ancient and recent history that this kind of spending binge inevitably leads to a tragic ending.

Here is a description of how government growth led to the fall of Rome:

> *The system of bureaucratic despotism, elaborated finally under Diocletian and Constantine, produced a tragedy in the truest sense, such as history has seldom exhibited; in which, by an inexorable fate, the claims of fanciful omnipotence ended in a humiliating paralysis of administration; in which determined effort to remedy social evils only aggravated them until they became unendurable; in which the best intentions of the central power were, generation after generation, mocked and defeated by irresistible laws of human nature.*
>
> -Samuel Dill, author of *Roman Society in the Last Century of the Western Empire*

Typically, nations that have traveled the course that we are now on have undergone a predictable cycle for financing their runaway budgets. The cycle has three stages that should sound familiar:

**Stage 1: Tax and Spend.** Government spending begins to outpace inflation and incomes. Politicians attempt to pay for the mushrooming government debt expenses by continuously raising taxes. But they run head-first into an iron law of economics, which is that the higher tax rates are lifted, the less additional revenues they yield. The tax and spend cycle also eventually collides with an iron law of politics: The electorate will tolerate higher taxes only up to a point; then they revolt.

**Stage 2: Borrow and Spend.** When raising taxes to keep pace with rising expenditures becomes politically futile, politicians turn to borrowing. And borrowing from the public and foreigners is an attractive short-term fix. But lawmakers soon discover that increasingly heavy borrowing imposes its own financial constraints. The debts have to be continuously repaid with interest, which adds to already-voluminous expenditures. This creates a demand for still more revenues, creating a fiscal treadmill whereby the government must run faster and faster just to stay in place. Creditors become increasingly uneasy about the credit worthiness of the government and its commitment to honoring its rising debts. The politicians soon discover that financing government through borrowing is an exercise in frustration—like the greyhounds racing around the dog track, trying to chase the ever-elusive mechanical rabbit.

**Stage 3: Inflate and Spend.** With debts piling up and the cost of borrowing rising inexorably, government often turns to its third option to pay for uncontrolled spending: Printing money. This inflation of the currency also carries with it an additional, short-term political benefit for government in that it not only raises revenues, it also reduces the real value of outstanding debt. Historically, however, the inflation spirals out of control and degenerates into hyperinflation. Ultimately the nation begins to either make draconian and painful reductions in public services and benefits, or is dragged into the abyss of complete financial insolvency.

This cycle has run its full course in countless Third World countries. In his best-selling book *Bankruptcy 1995*, Harry Figgie describes the spiralling debt and resulting hyperinflation in nations such as Argentina, Bolivia, and Brazil. In Argentina, a nation that had gained stature as one of the world's five wealthiest by the end of the first half of the twentieth century, massive public debts gave way to 500 and 600 percent inflation in the mid-1980s. These policies proved financially ruinous for the citizens of Argentina. The nation became so debt-plagued in the 1970s that inflation raged at 1,000 percent and more. Living standards in Argentina plummeted by more than 20 percent in the 1980s. This once-proud economic superpower fell to virtual Third World status by the late 1980s, thanks primarily to irresponsible government spending and lending behavior. It is only now, 15 years after the slide began, that Argentina has abandoned statist policies, and is showing signs of a genuine economic revival.

In America, we are now stuck in stage two of the fiscal cycle of national impoverishment. Through most of this century the government's *modus operandi* has been "tax and spend." A growing, prosperous nation was able to finance an ever-expanding public sector. Over the past twenty years, however, as the economy has failed to keep pace with government, the emphasis for financing government has been shifted to "borrow and spend."

$100 billion deficits of the 1970s have given way to $200 billion deficits in the 1980s, and now nearly $300 billion deficits in the 1990s.

The only real issue is whether we will cut government spending *now*, or whether we will wait till we enter into the third stage of the poverty cycle, and follow the path of the Argentinas and Brazils of the world.

## Recommended Reading

Figgie, Henry, *Bankruptcy 1995*

Friedman, Milton, "Why Government is the Problem." Hoover Institution, *Essays in Public Policy*, 1993

# 2

# Paradise Lost?

> *We Americans are so used to sustained economic growth in per-capita product that we tend to take it for granted—not realizing how exceptional growth of this magnitude is on the scale of human history.*
> -Simon Kuznets

The history of the United States is a history of spectacular economic progress perhaps unparalleled in all of human history. In fact, the advances have been so rapid that it's hard for Americans today to fully appreciate how far we have progressed in a very short time.

Throughout most of this century the American economy has grown at a real rate of between three and four percent per year. *Since 1900, real incomes of American families have doubled roughly every thirty years.* In other words, throughout this century, every generation of Americans has roughly succeeded in achieving a living standard that is twice that of their parents. Figure 2-1 shows that real per capita income has risen from about $3,000 in 1900 to over $20,000 today. *In less than one century, the standard of living in the United States has more than quadrupled.*

Similarly, the productivity and output of American workers has increased at a breathtaking pace. Manufacturing output per man-hour, for example, has increased sixfold since 1900. *In other words, it takes a worker 10 minutes today to produce what took an hour to produce at the turn of the century.* Figure 2-2 shows that in 1992

*Paradise Lost?*

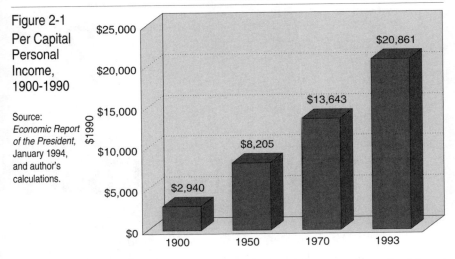

Figure 2-1 Per Capital Personal Income, 1900-1990

Source: *Economic Report of the President,* January 1994, and author's calculations.

the average American manufacturing worker produced at least 20 percent more in an hour than the average Japanese and German worker, and at least 25 percent more than the typical British worker.

This productivity increase has been bested only by the meteoric rise in the productivity of the American farmer. One hundred years ago, about half of the U.S. workforce was employed in agriculture and produced enough to eat for the 75 million Americans alive at that time. Now less than three percent of Americans are farmers, and they not only feed themselves and

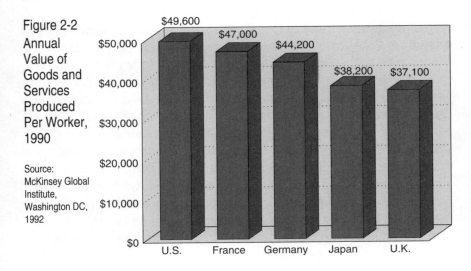

Figure 2-2 Annual Value of Goods and Services Produced Per Worker, 1990

Source: McKinsey Global Institute, Washington DC, 1992

## Paradise Lost?

the other 255 million of us, but also feed tens of millions more around the globe. The United States is unquestionably the breadbasket of the world.

To fully appreciate this achievement, consider that throughout human history the primary struggle of nations has been to feed themselves. It is a testament to the economic miracle of the United States' capitalist system that over the past several decades our government farm policy has been devoted to *reducing food production* in order to keep prices high and surpluses to a minimum. What a wonderful problem for a nation to have!

In this century the United States has developed a well-deserved reputation as the world's "job machine." From 1900 to 1980 the United States created an average of eight million new jobs each decade. In the 1980s the job machine shifted into over-drive; 18 million new jobs were created—mostly by record numbers of newly-formed small businesses. This was more jobs than were created in Japan, Korea, Germany, Sweden, or Great Britain. In fact, this was more jobs than were created in *all* those nations combined, *plus all of the rest of the nations of Europe.*

On top of creating tens of millions of new jobs, the American economy has also seen tremendous productivity increases. The share of the United States' gross domestic product (GDP) devoted to manufacturing everything from cars to chemicals and computers has *risen* from 20 percent in 1960 to 21 percent in 1970, and 23 percent in 1990. Some complain that manufacturing employment is down by more than two million in the past twenty years. But, as in agriculture, this is simply an indication that America is producing more and more goods, with fewer and fewer people.

Meanwhile, our material wealth is today far superior to what it was fifty and one hundred years ago, and far superior to the level achieved by other nations of the world. In 1950 there were about 30 cars per 100 persons; there are now more than 75. In 1950 telephone service reached just 62 percent of American homes, versus 95 percent today, nearly half of which have cordless phones. In 1950 television was still a novelty. Today more than 90 percent of American households own at least one *color* TV.

Even households that are considered "poor" in the United States today are relatively well-off in their standard of living, compared to households of even thirty years ago, and are rich compared to the average non-American. Poverty expert Robert Rector of the Heritage Foundation reports that *the median household income of Americans living in 1960 after adjusting for inflation was 10 percent* lower *than the median expenditures of Americans officially classified as "poor" today.* According to the U.S. Census Bureau:

- 40 percent of "poor" households own their own homes.
- More than half of poor families have air conditioning, own a car, and have a microwave oven.
- Ninety percent of the poor own a TV, and 30 percent own two color TVs.
- The average *poor* American household has twice the housing space as the average income Japanese household, and four times the living space of the average Russian household.
- Incredibly, an American family living right at the official poverty level is richer than 90 percent of the people living on earth today.

There is much truth to the adage, "If you have to be poor, America is a good place for it."

America's progress is not only evident in her economic accomplishments. Throughout history, life on earth for the vast majority of men and women has been, as Thomas Hobbes described the state of nature, "solitary, poor, nasty, brutish and short." People seldom lived beyond the age of 50. Children and their mothers routinely died at birth. Diseases and plagues and famines were capable of wiping out half of a nation's population. The essence of the human struggle has been to preserve and lengthen life.

In the twentieth century this pattern changed dramatically, as shown in Figure 2-3.

- In 1900 life expectancy in the United States was 47.
- In 1950 life expectancy was 68.
- In 1992 life expectancy was 76.

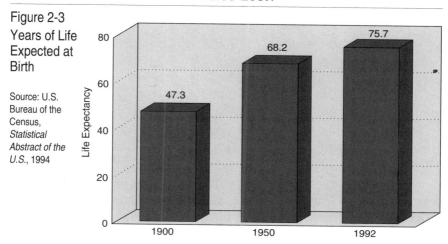

Figure 2-3
Years of Life Expected at Birth

Source: U.S. Bureau of the Census, *Statistical Abstract of the U.S.*, 1994

These longer life spans are the result of technological advances in farming, the launching of the era of modern medicine and its introduction of hundreds of new life-saving drugs (most of which were invented here in the United States), better diets, healthier lifestyles, and higher incomes.

An even more heartening triumph has been the rapid decline in infant mortality. A child born today is *four times* more likely to survive past his or her first year of life than a child born 100 years ago. This dramatic decline in infant mortality, together with longer life expectancy, represents a stunning triumph over premature or early death in the United States. And we have exported this triumph to every corner of the globe, where similar but less dramatic trends are being recorded. In fact, it is precisely because babies live after they are born, and because people are living longer lives, that the American population (and the world population for that matter) has steadily climbed in this century. How foolish that many American intellectuals mourn this trend, rather than celebrate it.

None of this is intended to trivialize the plight of the underclass or to imply that there are not serious economic and social inequities in the United States. But the central point here is that few nations have succeeded in improving the living standards of their citizens as well as the United States has in this century.

## ♦ Why America Grew Rich

Humanitarians often look around the world and see overwhelming and heartbreaking poverty and wonder why so many people are poor. They ask the wrong question. The normal human condition throughout history has been for human beings to be poor and to live at subsistence levels.

The question we ought to be asking is: *Why are there a few countries, most prominently the United States, that are rich?* What is the formula for economic success and prosperity?

In the United States the formula has been astonishingly simple. It is the combination of freedom, free enterprise, and limited government. Or, as John F. Kennedy put it in his famous address before the Economics Club of New York in 1962, the growth of the American economy in the twentieth century "demonstrates for all to see the power of freedom and the efficiency of free institutions."

More specifically, America's formula for economic success has included:

- Protection of private property rights;
- Rewards for hard work, enterprise, and initiative;
- Guarantees of basic political freedoms and human rights, such as freedom of speech and religion;
- Free trade of goods and services;
- The relatively unrestrained immigration of energetic and productive people who impart economic energies on those already here;
- A minimally burdensome and distortive tax system;
- Establishment of constitutional protections against the unchecked expansion of government.

It is an ethic that was best summarized by Thomas Jefferson in his famous line: "That government which governs best, governs least."

When other nations have adopted this formula of freedom and free enterprise, they have generally produced favorable results. Hong Kong is a good example of a place where limited government and virtually unrestrained free markets have produced a level of economic progress that would have been unimaginable thirty years ago. Meanwhile China, which began in 1950 at roughly the same economic starting point as Hong Kong, pursued precisely the opposite economic strategy—one of collectivism and statism. *By 1990 the average Hong Kong resident was about eight times wealthier than the average citizen of mainland China.*

## ◆ Killing the Goose that Lays the Golden Eggs

Nobel prize winning economist James M. Buchanan once described the free enterprise system in America as "the goose that lays the golden eggs." In recent years many Americans have begun to wonder whether the goose is still fertile.

In fact, a 1993 public opinion poll asked respondents to "compare the next generation's standard of living with your own." Thirty-one percent predicted that the next generation's living standard would be "better," and 61 percent said it would be "worse." In other words, most Americans fear we are going backwards.

The level of apprehension is understandable. Our recent economic performance has been highly disappointing. Under the past six presidents, from Richard Nixon to Bill Clinton (with the notable exception of Ronald Reagan), the doubling of income every generation that Americans have come to expect has abruptly ended.

America is suffering from a disturbing and widening "economic growth deficit." This deficit commands little public attention, but it has much more impact on the nation's long-term economic well-being than any other socioeconomic trend in America today. It is much more harmful, for example, than the well-publicized federal budget deficit.

What is an economic growth deficit? It is the difference between the U.S. economy's *potential* and *actual* performance.

◆ From 1974 to 1982 America's real annual economic growth rate hit the skids—slowing to about 2.2 percent, a sharp decline from the 3.5 to 4.0 percent pace averaged in the post-World War II era.

During the Reagan years the economy dramatically turned around, growth climbed back up to 3.3 percent, and incomes began to rise again. In large part this only recaptured the ground lost in the 1970s. *Real incomes are not much higher today than they were twenty years ago.*

But what is most disturbing to Americans today is the bleak outlook for the future. The post-Reagan years of the 1990s show all the signs of a 1970s replay. Through the first five years of the Bush-Clinton era, economic growth has been crawling ahead at an anemic two percent rate.

What is the practical significance of this growth deficit? Consider this:

- If the economy had grown over the past twenty years at the same pace it did in the 1940s, 1950s, and 1960s, today the average American household would have an income at least $12,000 higher than it is.

Just since the late 1980s, the growth deficit has lowered national output by $1.5 trillion dollars.

What does the growth deficit mean for the future? Over two, three, or four years, the difference between a four and a two percent growth rate is trivial—virtually unnoticeable. But notice in Figure 2-4 how the widening of the growth deficit has a dramatic compounding effect over time. After 25 years the American economy would be roughly 50 percent larger with the higher growth rate. After 50 years the American economy would be twice as large as under the slow-growth scenario. This is equivalent to the difference between the American standard of living today and the American standard of living fifty years ago.

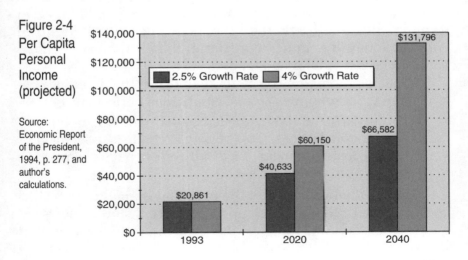

Figure 2-4
Per Capita Personal Income (projected)

Source: Economic Report of the President, 1994, p. 277, and author's calculations.

*Paradise Lost?*

## ♦ America Dragged Down

Most Americans have a romantic vision of the United States as being a country with a large, productive private sector supporting a relatively small, limited government. It is natural for us to think of America in these terms. After all, a limited government carrying out just a few tasks was precisely what our founding fathers established in precise terms in the U.S. Constitution. They regarded government as a necessary evil. In George Washington's words, "Government is, like fire, a dangerous servant and a fearful master."

Unfortunately, in the last 200 years the role of government serving the people has been reversed. *The reason that America finds itself on an economic downward spiral is that today, Washington, D.C. is taxing, spending, borrowing, mandating, decreeing, and regulating America to death.* The private sector—businesses, entrepreneurs, investors, workers, and families—is slowly suffocating under the weight of a relentlessly-expanding government.

There are countless indications of this growth of government:

- ♦ **Government Spending:** Real outlays at all levels of government have mushroomed from $1,650 per household in 1900, to $12,800 per household in 1960, to $24,000 per household in 1994 (see Figure 2-5). Throughout the first 150 years of this nation, government rarely spent more than 10 percent of total output. Today it spends nearly 40 percent of total output, and over 40 percent of national income (Table 2-4).

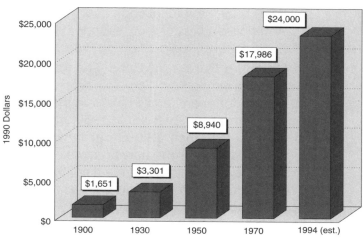

Figure 2-5
Real Total Government Spending/Household, 1900-1994

Source: *Facts and Figures on Government Finance*, various years; and both *State* and *Local Government Finances*, 1994 and earlier years.

## Table 2-1
### Spending as a Percent of National Income

| Year | Federal | State/Local | Total |
|------|---------|-------------|-------|
| 1930 | 3%      | 9%          | 12%   |
| 1940 | 13%     | 12%         | 25%   |
| 1950 | 20%     | 8%          | 28%   |
| 1960 | 22%     | 10%         | 32%   |
| 1970 | 24%     | 12%         | 36%   |
| 1980 | 26%     | 12%         | 38%   |
| 1990 | 28%     | 14%         | 42%   |

Source: Advisory Commission on Intergovernmental Relations, *Significant Features of Fiscal Federalism*, 1992.

- **The Tax Burden:** In 1900, taxes took one of every twelve dollars of the income of American workers. In 1950 taxes took one of every four dollars from American workers. In 1990 taxes consumed well over one of every three dollars of worker income.

- **Government Bureaucracy:** In 1900, four percent of the American workforce was employed by government. In 1950, 10 percent of the American workforce was employed by government. In 1990, 14 percent of Americans—one out of every seven workers—got their paychecks from government.

- **The Rise of the Welfare State:** Real total social welfare expenditures exploded from $10 billion in 1900 to $130 billion in 1950 to $1 trillion in 1992. That's more than the GDP of all but a handful of countries. Today one of every nine Americans collects food stamps. In New York City one of every *seven* residents is on welfare.

- **The Crushing Burden of Debt:** The national debt now stands at a towering $4 trillion. This represents a $62,000 debt burden for every family of four in the United States, up in real terms from $41,000 in 1950 after World War II, and up from less than $3,000 per family in 1900. The federal government alone now borrows almost $1 million per minute, every minute of every day 365 days a year. In the time it takes you to read this chapter, the government borrowed another $15 to $20 million.

*Paradise Lost?*

- **The Regulatory Stranglehold:** In 1935 there were 4,000 pages of regulations listed in the Federal Register. Today there are 65,000 pages of such regulations. The economic cost of complying with federal regulations is now estimated to be at least $400 billion per year. Economic regulation has the impact of a tax on every American worker. The amount of this tax is estimated to be about $4,000 for every household in the U.S. each year.

- **A Trillion Here and a Trillion There**

Some 30 years ago Senator Everett Dirksen described how Capital Hill politicians throw around money: "A billion here, and a billion there, and pretty soon you're talking about real money."

The federal budget is now right about $1.5 trillion, and the state and local governments spend roughly another trillion, bringing the total public expenditures to $2.5 trillion. Meanwhile, the federal debt has reached more than $4 trillion. The war on poverty has cost almost $5 trillion. Total federal liabilities are more than $10 trillion.

The problem is that one trillion is an unfathomably large number. Four trillion is simply four times an unfathomably large number. This explains why the release of the federal budget is not met with public outrage, but rather with a national shrug of dazed incomprehension.

Even the politicians themselves have become anesthetized to the large amounts of money they dole out each year and the fiscal devastation this causes. When President Clinton released his $1.52 trillion budget for 1995 (a $50 billion increase over the previous year), legislators applauded the President for being frugal and tightfisted. "A bare-bones budget," one Democratic Congressman called it. Senator Dirksen's axiom no longer applies on Capitol Hill. "A billion here and a billion there" is regarded as a long way off from spending real money. Spending one and a half trillion dollars is now praised as being frugal and tightfisted inside the Washington Beltway. Later, Congress passed a new anti-crime social welfare program entitled "An Ounce of Prevention." It's price tag: $1.3 billion. Yes, a billion three is now considered an ounce on Capitol Hill.

So to help arouse some genuine ire, outrage, and understanding, let's try to put a human face on a trillion dollars. A trillion dollars = $1,000,000,000,000.00. If you're counting, that's 12 zeroes to the left of

## Paradise Lost?

the decimal point. Here's one way to think about how much money that is: A trillion is a million million dollars. Most Americans today are lucky to earn $1 million in their lifetimes.

How does the size of the federal budget compare to the size of the entire economies of other nations? Figure 2-6 shows that the federal government spends more than all of the people of Germany. The U.S. government spends more than the entire GDP of Australia, China and Spain *combined*.

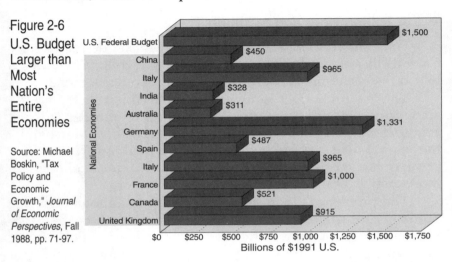

Figure 2-6
U.S. Budget Larger than Most Nation's Entire Economies

Source: Michael Boskin, "Tax Policy and Economic Growth," *Journal of Economic Perspectives*, Fall 1988, pp. 71-97.

One of the highest-paid workers in America today is basketball superstar Shaquille O'Neall, who reportedly earns about $25 million a season in salary and endorsements. He is rich beyond our wildest imaginations. But he would have to play 40,000 seasons before he earned $1 trillion. It would take 100,000 Shaquille O'Nealls—a standing-room only Rose Bowl full—to pay for one year of all federal, state and local spending in the U.S.

Here's an interesting experiment: What if we were to try to pay off the $4 trillion national debt by having Congress put one dollar every second into a special debt buy-down account. How many years would it take to pay off the debt? One million seconds is about 12 days. One billion seconds is roughly 32 years. But one trillion seconds is almost 32,000 years. So if Congress put dollar bills into this account for about the next 130,000 years—or roughly the amount of time that has passed since the Ice Age—the present debt would be paid off.

## Paradise Lost?

Even if we were to require Congress to put $100 a second into this debt reduction account, *it would still take well over 1,000 years to pay the debt down.* Translation: thanks to our spendthrift politicians, the federal government will be in the red for a long, long time.

Try this one on for size: Imagine a train of 50-foot boxcars crammed with one dollar bills. How long would the train have to be to carry the one-and-a-half-trillion dollars Congress spends each year? About $65 million can be stuffed into a train boxcar. The train would have to about 250 *miles* long to carry enough dollar bills to balance the federal budget. In other words, *to balance the budget you would need a train full of dollar bills that covers the entire Northeast corridor—from Washington, through Baltimore, Delaware, Philadelphia, New Jersey, and into New York City.*

Former Reagan Budget Director Jim Miller uses this analogy: Imagine a military jet flying at the speed of sound, reeling out a roll of dollar bills behind it. *It would have to fly for 14 years before it reeled out one trillion dollar bills.*

If you read every word in *The New York Times* every day for a year, you would have read nearly 30 million words. But you would have to do this for about 30,000 years before you would have read one trillion words. (Imagine the drudgery of having to read every word of *The New York Times* for more than 30,000 years!)

If you laid one dollar bills end to end, could you make a chain that stretches to the moon with one trillion? No problem. In fact, if you laid one trillion dollars end to end you it would stretch from the earth to the moon and back again 200 times before you ran out of dollar bills! *One trillion dollars would stretch nearly from the earth to the sun.*

Finally, with the $2.5 trillion that local, state and federal governments spend each year, *you could purchase all of the farmland in the United States, plus all of the assets of the Fortune 100 companies.*

In sum, one trillion is a lot of railroad cars, a lot of Shaquille O'Neall's, a lot of newspapers, a lot of trips to the moon, a lot of farmland, and most importantly, a lot of our hard-earned tax dollars to send to Washington—no matter how you stack it.

## ◆ More Government Then We Can Afford

Although many economists profess that they cannot explain the decline in U.S. economic growth in recent decades, Figure 2-7 is highly instructive. It compares the growth in annual output in the United States over the past 100 years with the annual size of government expenditures for these years. Growth has skidded from nearly four percent per year at the beginning of the century to 3.5 percent by around 1950 to just over two percent in recent years. Over this same time period, government spending as a share of national output climbed from 10 percent of national output in 1900 to 25 percent in 1950 to almost 40 percent today.

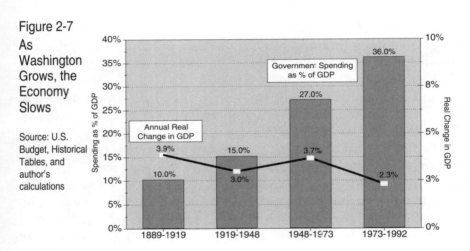

Figure 2-7
As Washington Grows, the Economy Slows

Source: U.S. Budget, Historical Tables, and author's calculations

Taxes may even have a more direct impact on the American economy than total spending. High tax rates on work, investment, and savings discourage all three. Economist John Skorburg and I discovered a remarkably consistent inverse relationship between government and economic performance over the period 1960 through 1992 even after taking into account other factors that might explain variations in economic performance. Our analysis estimates that the impact of taxes can be quantified as follows:

- ◆ Each one percentage point rise (fall) in the federal tax burden leads to a 1.25 percent reduction (increase) in economic growth in the following year.

- Each one percentage point rise (fall) in the federal tax burden leads to a 0.85 percentage point increase (reduction) in the unemployment rate.

Of course, some level of government is economically beneficial to provide basic services such as a military, law enforcement, roads and schools. The problems is that government is debilitating when it grows too bulky and onerous. So the critical economic question that Americans need to ask is: Has our government surpassed that turning point? Do we have more government than we can afford?

A recent study by Gerald Scully of the University of Texas (Dallas) shows that we do. Prof. Scully attempted to quantify the economically optimal level of government for the United States. In other words, what is the size of government that maximizes economic growth? Examining U.S. data from 1919 to 1987, Scully estimates that the American economy has prospered most when the federal government consumes about 12 percent of national output. According to Scully, below this size, government is possibly smaller than required to maximize growth. Above it, the benefits of additional government spending are outweighed by the losses of private sector activity. His conclusion is worth repeating:

> *On the basis of the empirical estimates, a size of the fiscal enterprise above about 12 percent of GNP imposes a "growth tax" on its citizens. This growth tax is higher the larger the growth tax is relative to the growth maximizing tax rate . . . . What is particularly pernicious about a growth tax is that it is unobserved. There is no constituency of opposition to the growth tax.*

Scully calculates that in 1987 when taxes were 18.1 percent of GNP the "growth tax" was roughly five percent of GNP. At a level of taxes and spending of well-over 20 percent of GNP today, the growth tax is approaching 10 percent of GDP. In other words, Americans are some $600 billion poorer each year, the equivalent of nearly $6,000 per household, simply because Congress is giving us more government than Americans can afford.

## ◆ A $10 Trillion Federal Budget?

What is frightening is that government will continue to grow in America unless citizens prevent it. If we simply stay on the course we have followed for the past forty years and do not radically change the direction and scope of government, then Washington will continue its relentless and ruinous expansion:

- ◆ The federal government will have a $2 trillion dollar budget by the year 2000; and a $10 trillion budget by the year 2020. In today's dollars, the federal budget will reach $4 trillion in the next 25 years, as shown in Figure 2-8. In real dollars the federal government will have spent more in 2020 than it did in the first two hundred years of America's history!

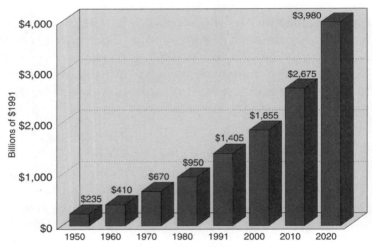

Figure 2-8 Projected Federal Spending in Constant Dollars

- ◆ Today's $250 billion deficits will soon seem like a minor inconvenience compared to what lies ahead as federal spending follows its dangerous path. In constant 1990 dollars we will have a $400 billion deficit by the year 2000; a $750 billion deficit in 2010; and a $1.5 trillion deficit in 2020.
- ◆ If the politicians opt to pay for this massive spending buildup through taxes, then the typical American family's tax bill after adjusting for inflation will rise not by 10, 20, or even 50 percent, but by 150 percent!

## ◆ Still the Land of the Free?

Americans have long viewed government as a benign force that protects the public welfare. That may have been true 100 or even 50 years ago, but today government is so large and meddlesome that it is undermining the public welfare. More than any hostile foreign nation, more than any criminal, more than any natural disaster, our own United States government today is the single greatest threat to our economic security and basic freedoms.

Our economic problem is not that the American formula for success—the formula that created a run of economic progress unmatched in human history—does not work anymore. It's that the formula has been abandoned, and our rights and freedoms have been usurped in favor of a new political doctrine of greed, envy, dependency, entitlement, and paternalism.

Washington has slain the goose that lays the golden eggs.

### Recommended Reading

*America: What Went Right in the 1980s*, Pacific Research Institute, San Francisco, 1994.

Hazlett, Henry, *Economics in One Lesson*

Friedman, Milton, *Capitalism and Freedom*

# 3

# Other People's Money

> *I'm going to build me the God-damnedest, biggest, chromium-platedest, formaldehyde-stinkingest free public hospital the all-Father ever let live. Boy, I tell you, I'm going to have a cage of canaries in every room that can sing Italian grand opera, and there ain't going to be a nurse hasn't won a beauty contest and every doorknob will be eighteen carat gold, and by God, every bedpan will have a Swiss music box attachment to play "Turkey in the Straw" or the "Sextet from Lucia," take your pick.*
>
> Willie Stark, in Robert Penn Warren's
> *All the King's Men*

The first budget of the United States called for federal spending of $750,000. Oh, how things have changed! In the current trillion and a half dollar budget, $750,000 would not even show up as a rounding error.

### ◆ The Federal Spending Juggernaut

How much money does the U.S. government spend each year? Figure 3-1 shows the expansion of the federal budget from

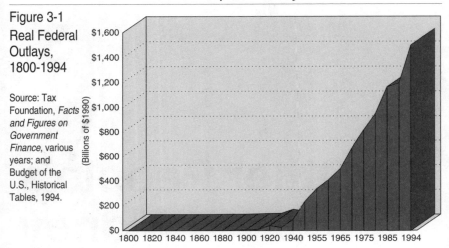

Figure 3-1
Real Federal Outlays, 1800-1994

Source: Tax Foundation, *Facts and Figures on Government Finance*, various years; and Budget of the U.S., Historical Tables, 1994.

1800 to 1994. The steep ascent underscores the ten-thousandfold explosion of real federal spending since Thomas Jefferson was President in 1800. The graph rockets upward particularly since 1930, when the Constitutional protections against runaway government first began to erode. Federal outlays have climbed from $100 million in 1800 to $600 million in 1850, to $8.3 billion in 1900, to $235 billion in 1950, to $1.5 trillion today. *If federal outlays had been restrained to the inflation rate over just the past 20 years, America would now have a $250 billion budget surplus, rather than a $250 billion deficit.*

To put this growth rate of spending in a more understandable context, in 1850 it took the federal government almost two years to spend $1 billion (1992 dollars). In 1900 it took almost a month and a half on average to spend $1 billion. By 1950 it took roughly one day and a half to spend $1 billion, but now Uncle Sam spends $1 billion on average every six hours!

Of course, the nation is much larger and more populous today than in earlier periods, so one would expect government also to be bigger. Figure 3-2 shows the per capita level of federal spending over time. Even when adjusting for the growth in population and inflation, government expenditures have mushroomed:

- The federal government spent $20 per person in 1800.
- The federal government spent $110 per person in 1900.
- The federal government spent $5,030 per person in 1994.

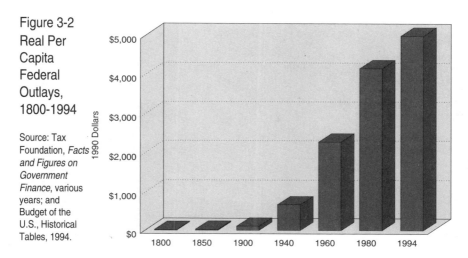

Figure 3-2
Real Per Capita Federal Outlays, 1800-1994

Source: Tax Foundation, *Facts and Figures on Government Finance*, various years; and Budget of the U.S., Historical Tables, 1994.

Bear in mind that this does not include any of the "back door" spending by Congress such as the costs of regulations and mandates. If these costs were included, the per capita cost of the federal government would be close to $10,000 per person.

One of the most meaningful ways of measuring the burden of government is by looking at expenditures as a share of total economic output. One might argue that the government spends more money today because the American economy has grown so much larger than in earlier periods. If the state is consuming the same proportion of total output in two periods, then the economic burden of paying for its activities is roughly the same even if expenditures are much larger in the later period. Unfortunately, Figure 3-3 shows that federal spending is not simply keeping pace with economic growth—it is far outpacing economic growth.

- ♦ In 1900 the federal government consumed less than five percent of total output.
- ♦ In 1950 the federal government consumed roughly 15 percent of total output.
- ♦ In 1993 the federal government consumed about 24 percent of national output.

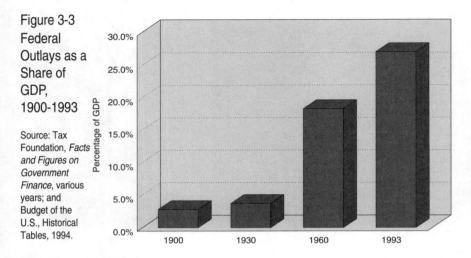

Figure 3-3
Federal Outlays as a Share of GDP, 1900-1993

Source: Tax Foundation, *Facts and Figures on Government Finance*, various years; and Budget of the U.S., Historical Tables, 1994.

◆ **National Defense**

The single most important activity of the federal government is to provide for the national defense. A nation spends as much as is necessary to protect its borders and its citizens from foreign aggression. In the first federal budget, almost three-quarters of all expenditures were for the army and navy (remember, almost all the enumerated spending powers in the Constitution involved the military). Since then, the share of federal expenditures devoted to the military has been steadily shrinking—except, of course, during times of war—over the past two hundred years (see Figure 3-4).

- Defense spending was 55 percent of federal outlays in 1800.
- Defense spending constituted 34 percent of federal outlays in 1900.
- Defense spending now constitutes 21 percent of federal outlays, with the percentage expected to shrink to 15 percent by the year 2000.

Many Americans believe that the reason America now faces a huge budget deficit is the Reagan defense build-up of the early 1980s. This is complete nonsense. The truth is that defense spending, even at the height of the Reagan build-up, reached only 6.5 percent of GDP, and comprised only 30 percent of the budget. By contrast, the *average* level of defense spending during the entire

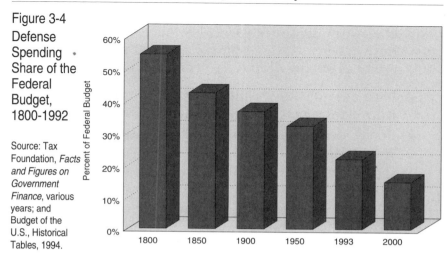

Figure 3-4
Defense Spending Share of the Federal Budget, 1800-1992

Source: Tax Foundation, *Facts and Figures on Government Finance*, various years; and Budget of the U.S., Historical Tables, 1994.

Cold War period was 8.4 percent of GDP and 40 percent of the budget. Figure 3-5 shows that during Kennedy's presidency, the U.S. spent about 10 percent of GDP on defense. Defense outlays will soon be down to 4% of GDP—the lowest burden of Pentagon spending since the year before America entered World War II. National defense is not the driving force of our current reckless fiscal policies—it is a casualty of those policies.

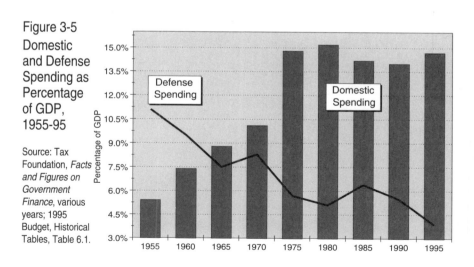

Figure 3-5
Domestic and Defense Spending as Percentage of GDP, 1955-95

Source: Tax Foundation, *Facts and Figures on Government Finance*, various years; 1995 Budget, Historical Tables, Table 6.1.

## Other People's Money

One of Washington's best kept secrets is that Reagan's celebrated defense build-up ended in 1986. Since then, real Pentagon spending has been slashed by more than 20 percent. Here are some examples of how deep these spending cuts have been:

- The cumulative dollar savings from the defense draw-down since 1987 has exceeded $300 billion.
- Today, defense spending comprises a smaller share of the total budget than at any time in 200 years.
- Defense spending in real dollars will be lower in 1995 than it was in 1955.

There is virtually no other area of the budget that has *declined* over the past forty years. It is a sham to blame today's $250 billion deficits on military spending when such spending is lower today than when the era of triple digit deficits began.

### ◆ Whatever Happened to the Peace Dividend?

One of the most troubling trends in the federal budget is that although *defense* spending is falling rapidly, *deficit* spending is not. Rather, the "peace dividend" from the Cold War is being spent on arts subsidies, entitlement expansions, small business loans, Amtrak, congressional salaries, maple syrup research, and a myriad of other civilian programs. From 1987 to 1994, real defense spending has been cut by $75 billion. But spending on everything else in the

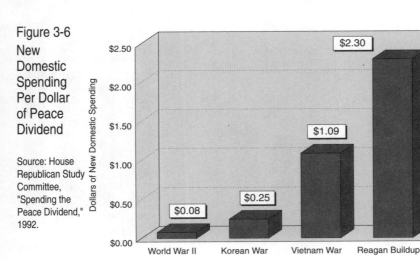

Figure 3-6
New Domestic Spending Per Dollar of Peace Dividend

Source: House Republican Study Committee, "Spending the Peace Dividend," 1992.

## Other People's Money

budget has risen by over $200 billion over the same period. In fact, Figure 3-6 shows that Congress's propensity to spend the "peace dividend" has increased after every war.

- After World War II the government spent eight cents of every peace dividend dollar.
- After the Korean War Congress spent 25 cents of each peace dividend dollar.
- After the Vietnam War, Congress spent $1.09 of every dollar of military savings.
- After the Cold War, Congress has spent $2.30 of every peace dividend dollar.

With the end of the Cold War, fiscal prudence would seem to dictate that as we draw down military expenditures, we use those savings to cut the high tax rates that went to pay for the military build-up. Instead, there will be no dividend for taxpayers and no reduction in the debt. Congress has already spent the money twice over on entitlements and a grab bag of other domestic programs.

### ◆ Domestic Spending

The flip side of this steady reduction of defense expenditures as a share of the budget is an expansion in spending on civilian programs. Figure 3-7 contrasts the rise in domestic expenditures over the past 40 years with the fall in defense outlays. For every dollar of defense spending in 1955, the domestic program spent 50

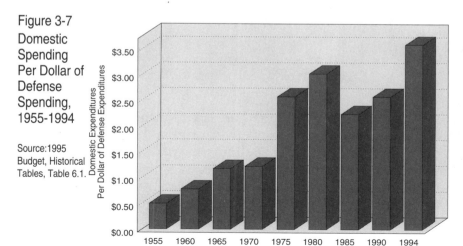

Figure 3-7
Domestic Spending Per Dollar of Defense Spending, 1955-1994

Source: 1995 Budget, Historical Tables, Table 6.1.

cents. Now, for every dollar of defense spending, domestic agencies spend close to $4. Although there were modest spending reductions on selected domestic programs in the Reagan years, in 1993 the budget for almost every major domestic area of the budget was at an all time high. There simply can be no doubt that spending on civilian programs is responsible for our fiscal crisis today.

## *Agriculture*

What was the fastest growing agency in the federal budget during the 1980s? No, it was not the Pentagon. It was the U.S. Department of Agriculture. The budget for farm programs ballooned from $4 billion in 1980 to $30 billion in 1986. Most of the funds went to subsidize cotton, wheat, wool and mohair, sugar, corn, and even honey. Most of the rest went for food stamps. Figure 3-8 shows the meteoric rise of U.S. Department of Agriculture expenditures since 1900.

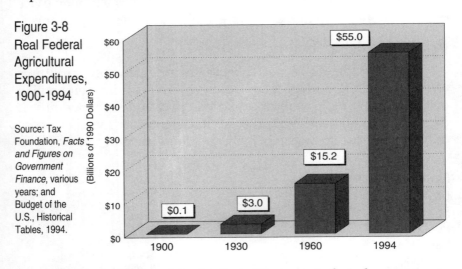

Figure 3-8
Real Federal Agricultural Expenditures, 1900-1994
(Billions of 1990 Dollars)

Source: Tax Foundation, *Facts and Figures on Government Finance*, various years; and Budget of the U.S., Historical Tables, 1994.

The Department of Agriculture is a case study in how government programs grow beyond their original missions. The first federal appropriation for agriculture was made in 1839 when Congress approved $1,000 for the collection of agriculture statistics. By 1932 the agency was spending $250 million a year for studies of worms, home cooking hints, gardening techniques, cattle tick services, and hundreds of other questionable programs.

The massive farm subsidy programs of today are a legacy of Franklin Roosevelt's administration. These farm subsidies were used to pay farmers **not** to plant. These programs cannot even be justified on income redistribution grounds. Forty percent of farm subsidies go to farms with incomes over $100,000, and seventy percent goes to farmers with incomes of over $50,000. Farm programs take income from middle-income consumers and give it to America's wealthiest farmers. *More than 85% of subsidies go to farmers with a net worth of nearly half a million dollars.*

## *Housing*

Substantial federal housing programs were first launched in the post-World War II period, and Figure 3-9 shows their stunning growth. Huge public housing projects were the first physical signs of the "war on poverty." They quickly became unlivable centers of crime, drugs, teen pregnancy, juvenile delinquency, and hopelessness—a visible testament to the failures of the "war on poverty."

*The New York Times* recently wrote that there is a general consensus that the billions of dollars spent to segregate the poor in huge public housing projects "distinctly failed."

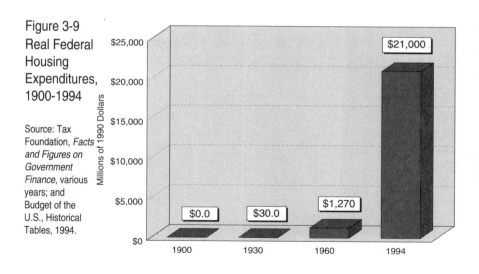

Figure 3-9
Real Federal Housing Expenditures, 1900-1994

Source: Tax Foundation, *Facts and Figures on Government Finance*, various years; and Budget of the U.S., Historical Tables, 1994.

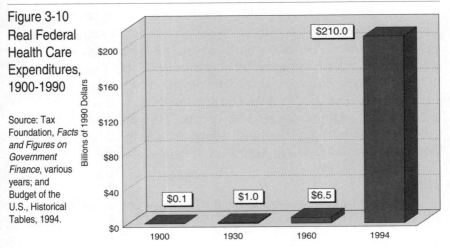

Figure 3-10
Real Federal Health Care Expenditures, 1900-1990

Source: Tax Foundation, *Facts and Figures on Government Finance*, various years; and Budget of the U.S., Historical Tables, 1994.

## Health Care

No category of the federal budget has grown as fast as health care expenditures. Figure 3-10 shows the enormous increase in federal health care spending in this century. In 1900 the federal government spent $100 million on health care (1990 dollars); in 1994 it spent $210 *billion* dollars. Virtually all of this growth has occurred since the mid-1960s when Medicare and Medicaid were launched.

Figure 3-11 shows the growth of Medicaid from 1970. In thirty years the program has grown ten-fold. When Medicaid

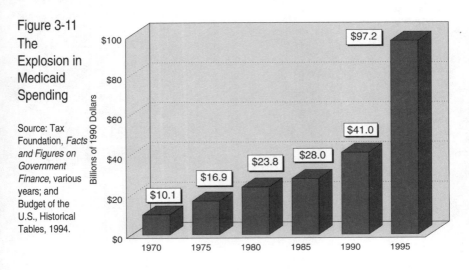

Figure 3-11
The Explosion in Medicaid Spending

Source: Tax Foundation, *Facts and Figures on Government Finance*, various years; and Budget of the U.S., Historical Tables, 1994.

was created, government actuaries predicted that it would cost about $25 billion by 1995. They were off by a factor of four. Similarly, Congress predicted that by 1990 Medicare for the elderly would cost only $12 billion. Instead it cost $107 billion.

## *Education*

For the past three decades American taxpayers have been pouring money into the public school system with almost no encouraging signs that this money is buying better education for our children.

In 1910 the U.S. spent about $500 per student versus $5,800 today. Though per-student expenditures have climbed steadily over the past 120 years, the most dramatic increases in education expenditures have occurred over the past four decades.

- In 1950 the U.S. education system was the best in the world. The U.S. spent $880 per student.
- By 1970 per student U.S. education expenditures had more than tripled.
- By 1992 per student U.S. education expenditures nearly doubled again to $5,850.

The U.S. Department of Education was created in 1978. Judging from all measures of academic performance, our children have suffered ever since. Real federal education expenditures, despite a slight slowdown in the early 1980s, have grown from $5 billion to $30 billion in the past thirty years.

Figure 3-12
Per-Pupil Educational Expenditures vs. SAT Scores

Source: U.S. Dept. of Education, *Digest of Education Statistics, 1992*, Table 121, p. 125, and Table 156, p. 159.

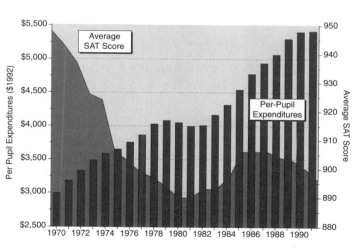

## ◆ A Trillion Dollars of Entitlements

It is impossible to talk about the growth of government in America without addressing the relentless growth of entitlements. The truth is that today it is a great challenge in the United States to find some citizen who does not receive a check from the government for one reason or another. It's not just the proverbial widows and orphans who are receiving government handouts: Every week the federal government sends out tens of billions of dollars of payments to:

- Farmers for growing (and for not growing) crops;
- Veterans for serving in the military;
- The unemployed for being unemployed;
- About one in nine households to pay for food;
- Students to pay for college;
- The elderly for being retired;
- The elderly and poor to pay for health care;
- Mothers for having children out of wedlock;
- Low income families to pay for rent;
- Homeowners to guarantee the mortgage; and on and on.

Fifty years ago most of today's entitlement programs didn't even exist. This is demonstrated by Figure 3-13, which shows the trend in federal, state, and local government social welfare outlays.

- In 1900 the government spent $10 billion on welfare.
- In 1960 the government spent $233 billion on welfare.
- In 1990 the government spent $1.004 trillion on welfare.

On the federal level, transfer programs are starting to subsume everything else in the budget. Entitlements constituted roughly 10 percent of the federal budget in 1930, 23 percent in 1960, but 53 percent today.

Transfer payments are not just for poor people. Most of our entitlement dollars are for Social Security, Medicare, and other programs that have come to be called "middle class entitlements." Only one in six government entitlement dollars goes to families with incomes below the poverty level. Incredibly, according to the National Taxpayers Union, in 1991 the average entitlement benefit to households under with incomes under $10,000 was less than the average

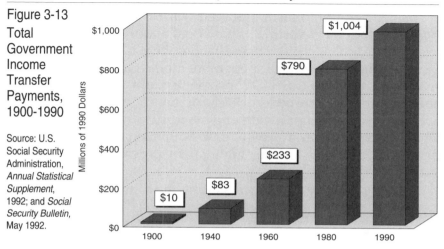

Figure 3-13
Total Government Income Transfer Payments, 1900-1990

Source: U.S. Social Security Administration, *Annual Statistical Supplement*, 1992; and *Social Security Bulletin*, May 1992.

benefit to households with incomes over $100,000. The poor got $5,333 per household and the over $100,000 crowd got $5,365. Even the affluent are cashing in on Uncle Sam's largesse these days.

◆ **The Welfare Industry**

No one should conclude from the preceding paragraph that we are somehow being stingy toward the poor. If we examine anti-poverty programs, such as AFDC, Medicaid, food stamps, public housing, unemployment compensation, and public aid, we find that in 1993 total federal, state, and local welfare payments exceeded $200 billion. As Figure 3-14 shows, this was up from about $10 billion in 1930 and $53 billion in 1970.

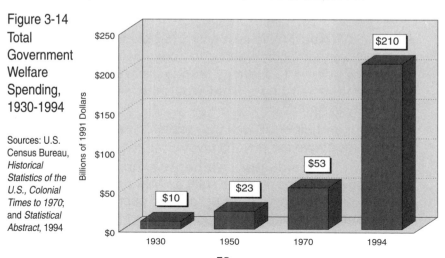

Figure 3-14
Total Government Welfare Spending, 1930-1994

Sources: U.S. Census Bureau, *Historical Statistics of the U.S., Colonial Times to 1970*; and *Statistical Abstract*, 1994

Since Lyndon Johnson declared war on poverty in the mid-1960s, the federal government has spent almost $5 trillion trying to eradicate it. That's more than 50 times what it cost NASA to put a man on the moon. We've spent more money on the War on Poverty than the entire U.S. GDP in 1985. In California, the average household on welfare collects $1,400 a month in benefits. In New York City welfare families are eligible for $26,940 a year in benefits. This gives them a pre-tax cash-equivalent income of more than $40,000 for not working, higher than 95 percent of the people in the world today.

Yet the poverty problem is getting much worse, not better.

- We still have roughly 30 million Americans who live below the poverty level—and the numbers are rising.
- In New York City, one of every seven residents is on welfare. In California, one in five AFDC recipients has been on the program for more than eight years. Welfare has become a way of life. The ratio of workers to welfare recipients in California is expected to drop to 3 to 1 by the end of the decade.
- In the inner cities, as many as 80 percent of all black births are now to single mothers.

Despite the huge outlays on anti-poverty programs, this spending has done amazingly little to reduce poverty. One reason for this lack of success is that welfare spending is badly misallocated.

- In 1990 government anti-poverty spending equaled $184 billion.
- In 1990 it would have cost only $75 billion to bring every family with an income below the poverty level up above that benchmark. Hence, taxpayers were spending two-and-a-half times what would be needed to end poverty in America.
- More than half of all welfare recipients had *pre-welfare incomes* above the poverty level.
- The welfare industry intercepts a huge portion of anti-poverty funds. In cities such as Milwaukee, there are now 62 separate welfare programs, each with its own bureaucratic costs.

## Other People's Money

Sadly, there is much truth to the adage that we fought a war on poverty, and poverty won.

### ◆ Red Ink Rising

Another rapidly growing component of the federal deficit is interest on the national debt. Figure 3-15 shows the rising cost of paying for the national debt.

- ◆ In 1900 interest on the debt was less than $1 billion.
- ◆ In 1960 interest on the debt was $30 billion.
- ◆ In 1994 interest on the debt reached $200 billion.

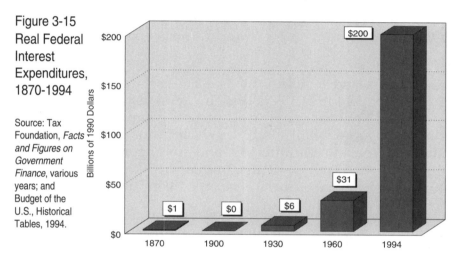

Figure 3-15
Real Federal Interest Expenditures, 1870-1994

Source: Tax Foundation, *Facts and Figures on Government Finance*, various years; and Budget of the U.S., Historical Tables, 1994.

Interest is now the third largest item in the budget behind Social Security and national defense. If current trends continue, interest payments will soon be the single biggest item in the budget.

Interest expenses are climbing, of course, because of the runaway national debt. Figure 3-16 shows:

- ◆ In 1900 each family of four carried a $2,600 share of the national debt.
- ◆ In 1950, shortly after World War II, each family of four carried an $40,000 share of the national debt.
- ◆ Today each family of four carries a $64,000 share of the national debt. This is the equivalent of every American family carrying around a $64,000 second mortgage.

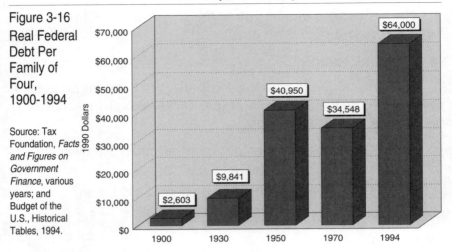

Figure 3-16
Real Federal Debt Per Family of Four, 1900-1994

Source: Tax Foundation, *Facts and Figures on Government Finance*, various years; and Budget of the U.S., Historical Tables, 1994.

What is frightening is that the official debt statistics cited above are severely *understated*. Our national debt is reported as $4.5 trillion, but in fact is potentially more than three times that large. The National Taxpayers Union has computed what it calls the Taxpayers Liability Index—which includes all of the outstanding loans, commitments, and contingencies of the U.S. government. A large portion of this liability is, of course, the unfunded obligations of Social Security. Others include:

- The government has $5.4 trillion of outstanding loans and loan guarantees, to farmers, businessmen, homeowners, and students.
- The government has insured about $5.8 trillion worth of pensions and other financial assets—including bank deposits and most of the private pensions of large American companies.
- The government has almost $500 billion in future unfulfilled contractual obligations.

Figure 3-17 shows that the total Taxpayer Liability Index hit $16.8 trillion in 1993 and is growing by about $1 trillion in real terms every three to four years. This is equal to about $150,000 for every American household. Your second mortgage just got considerably heavier.

## Other People's Money

Figure 3-17
Taxpayer's
Liability
Index:
Total
Potential
Financial
Obligations
of the U.S.
Government

Source: National
Taxpayers Union,
*Dollars & Sense*,
Dec. 1993/Jan.
1994, p. 8.

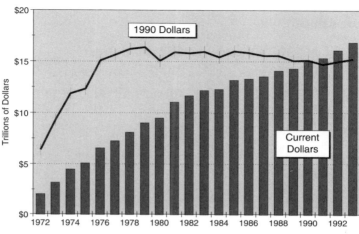

### ◆ States Join in the Spending Splurge

Because almost all cities and states have to abide by the discipline of balanced budget requirements, they have not had the luxury of financing spending through massive borrowing in the way that Washington has. Moreover, because state and local governments are "closer to the people" (and the taxpayers who fund their activities), they have tended to be somewhat more restrained in their spending habits than the federal government (see table below).

|      | Spending as a Percentage of National Income |               |       |
| ---- | ------- | ------------- | ----- |
| Year | Federal | State & Local | Total |
| 1930 | 3%      | 9%            | 12%   |
| 1940 | 13%     | 12%           | 25%   |
| 1950 | 20%     | 8%            | 28%   |
| 1960 | 22%     | 10%           | 32%   |
| 1970 | 24%     | 12%           | 36%   |
| 1980 | 26%     | 12%           | 38%   |
| 1990 | 28%     | 14%           | 42%   |

Source: Advisory Commission on Intergovernmental Relations

Figure 3-18 shows the real per capita levels of state expenditures since 1900.

- In 1900 states spent $32 per person.
- In 1950 states spent $470 per person.
- In 1993 states spent roughly $2,500 per person.

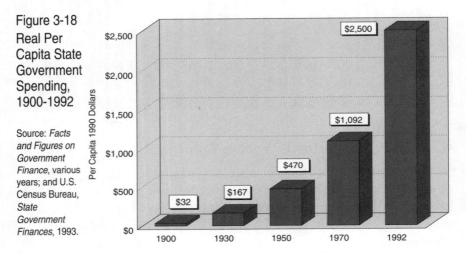

Figure 3-18
Real Per Capita State Government Spending, 1900-1992

Source: *Facts and Figures on Government Finance*, various years; and U.S. Census Bureau, *State Government Finances*, 1993.

The 1980s were years of unprecedented spending growth in state capitals from Albany to Sacramento. "In the 1980s, money rolled into the states in wheelbarrows and there was little incentive to put the champagne bottles down and manage nickels," concedes Connecticut Governor Lowell Weicker. Unfortunately, his assessment is right on the mark. Between 1982 and 1992, thanks to the surging national economy and revenue rich state coffers, state budgets climbed from $300 billion to $450 billion—that's a 50 percent real increase. In some states, the real spending increases were much faster:

- In California and Massachusetts state spending climbed by 65 percent.
- In New Jersey the budgets grew by 80 percent.
- The champion big spenders were Arizona, Connecticut, and Florida, all of whose budgets grew by 90 percent or more.

## Other People's Money

In recent years, in a kind of *reverse federalism*, the states have been ordered by the feds to spend money on all sorts of activities, from drug prevention, to homelessness, to health care for the indigent. These mandates have been an albatross around the necks of states and cities. But the budget expansions of the 1980s were not confined to federal mandates, as discretionary programs grew at a furious pace as well. Consider some of the waste and extravagance in state government over the last decade:

- California spent $16 million a year on an arts council, $4 million a year for a Board of Cosmetology, and $3 million for an Iceberg Lettuce Commission.
- New York's welfare bureaucracy spent $1,100 a year just to administer an AFDC case.
- In the 1980s, North Carolina's ratio of teachers to non-teaching employees on the school payrolls fell from two-to-one to one-to-one, after pouring state funds into the education budget.
- In perhaps the granddaddy of all boondoggles, the state of Virginia recently helped Fairfax County build a palatial $100 million government center, complete with granite floors imported from Finland, glass elevators, and a $30,000 conference table made of rare mahogany imported from South America.

### ◆ Spending in City Hall

Although it is conventional wisdom in Washington these days that our cities are starved for funds, the truth is that over the past several decades local governments have followed a spending path which, unfortunately, closely resembles that of the states. This is documented in Figure 3-19, which shows:

- In 1900 cities spent $200 per resident.
- In 1950 cities spent $600 per resident.
- In 1990 cities spent $2,400 per resident.

In other words, for every dollar that cities spent per resident in 1900 they spent $2.30 in 1950 and $8.50 in 1990.

It is a widespread myth that the affluent suburbs spend more money and have fatter budgets than large inner-cities. Cit-

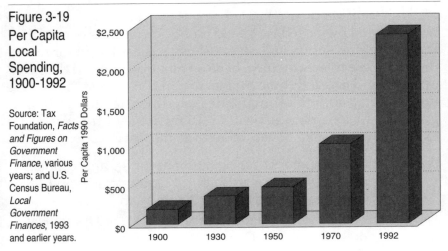

Figure 3-19
Per Capita Local Spending, 1900-1992

Source: Tax Foundation, *Facts and Figures on Government Finance*, various years; and U.S. Census Bureau, *Local Government Finances*, 1993 and earlier years.

ies with over half-a-million population spend roughly $1,200 per person today, versus expenditures of $550 per resident in communities with less than 75,000 residents. Even excluding health, education, and welfare expenditures, where funding responsibilities vary among states, per capita expenditures were $1,636 in San Francisco, $1,328 in Detroit, $1,341 in Philadelphia, and $1,454 in Boston. New York City, of course, is in a spending zone all its own with per capita expenditures of $2,058.

### ◆ The Most Government Money Can Buy

Now we can combine the spending totals at the federal, state, and local levels to get a comprehensive fiscal snapshot of government in the United States at various periods of history. In 1900 government in America was still comparatively lean and efficient. At that time total federal, state, and local expenditures were $26 billion. Americans now support a $2.5 trillion government, as shown if Figure 3-20. This is nearly a one hundred-fold increase in government in this century—which is why we can say that government is America's number 1 growth industry.

But as we know, trillions of dollars are hard to comprehend. So let's examine snapshots of government spending on a per-household basis and as a share of GDP. Figures 3-21 and 3-22 show that:

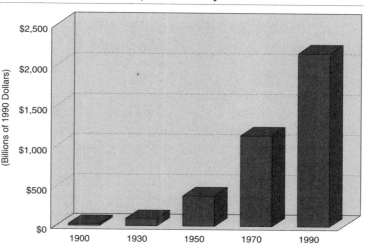

Figure 3-20
Combined Local, State and Federal Spending, 1900-1995

Source: *Facts and Figures on Government Finance*, various years; and both *State* and *Local Government Finances*, 1993 and earlier years.

- Government accounted for nine percent of national output in 1900. Today it accounts for 37 percent.
- Government spent $1,650 for every household in 1900, and $8,940 per household in 1950. Today it spends $24,000 per household. Again, remember this does not include any of the indirect costs of government, such as regulation.

Very few American families think they are getting $24,000 worth of goods and services from government each year. Even fewer probably believe that they can get twice the quality of gov-

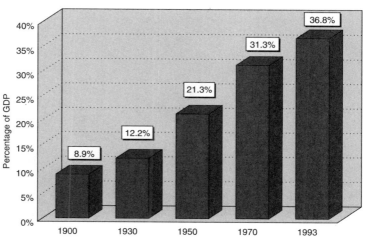

Figure 3-21
Total Government Outlays as a Share of GDP, 1900-1992

Source: *Facts and Figures on Government Finance*, various years; and both *State* and *Local Government Finances*, 1993

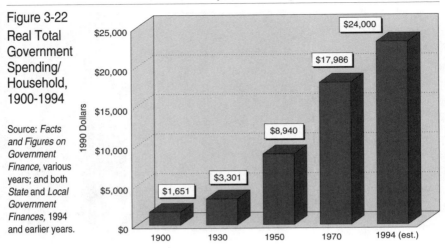

Figure 3-22
Real Total Government Spending/ Household, 1900-1994

Source: *Facts and Figures on Government Finance*, various years; and both *State* and *Local Government Finances*, 1994 and earlier years.

ernment services today compared to 30 years ago—although government costs twice as much. Indeed, most Americans think the schools are worse, the streets are less safe and clean, and the quality of other core services of government have deteriorated. It seems reasonably safe to conclude that at a cost of $24,000 a year, government is a remarkably bad deal.

A recent public opinion poll confirms this assessment. Americans were asked the following question: How many cents do you think are wasted out of every dollar that government spends?

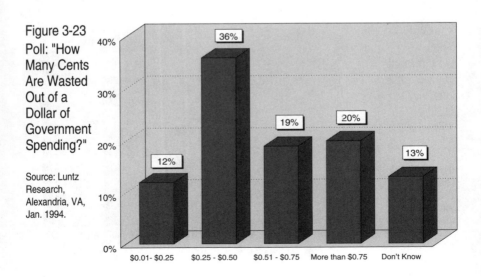

Figure 3-23
Poll: "How Many Cents Are Wasted Out of a Dollar of Government Spending?"

Source: Luntz Research, Alexandria, VA, Jan. 1994.

The results, as shown in Figure 3-23, were hardly a ringing endorsement for the value of government programs. Three out of four Americans believe that government wastes *at least* 25 cents of every dollar spent. Almost four of ten believe that more than 50 cents of every federal dollar is wasted.

### ◆ Conclusion

The late social scientist C. Northcote Parkinson, the man who stated "Parkinson's Law," often warned of the consequences of the ever-encroaching modern-day state. The first stage of the collapse of empires, he wrote, was the consolidation of political and financial power under "one government machine into which all problems are fed and from which all wisdom is to emerge."

"Without any conscious thought the politicians have come to the conclusion that the interests of the next generation can be, and should be ignored," Parkinson lamented. He asked of our lawmakers: "Can they not sense the disasters toward which they are heading? Can they not perceive what the future holds for them and for us?"

Apparently, in America, the politicians cannot.

### Recommended Reading

Beck, James M., *Our Wonderland of Bureaucracy*. MacMillan, 1933

Higgs, Robert, *Crisis and Leviathan*. Oxford University Press, 1990

Miller, James, *Fix the U.S. Budget*. Hoover Press, 1994

# 4

# Feeding The Beast

*What is the difference between
a taxidermist and a tax collector?
The taxidermist takes only your skin.*
-Mark Twain

The American Revolution was perhaps the greatest tax revolt in world history. No single event of the revolutionary era stands more fixed in the American psyche than the Boston Tea Party: A raucous colonial rebellion against the levying of heavy and unjust taxation by a distant ruler. Today, taxes at every level of government are much higher than could have been imagined in colonial days. In 1994, government in America surpassed an inglorious milestone: For the first time ever, the tax collectors took in more than $2 trillion of our money. Ironically, we have much higher taxation *with* representation than what was imposed on us *without* representation. Even worse, these taxes have become the lubricant of a massive and intrusive government sector—just what the Revolution was fought against.

◆ **Calculating Your Tax Bill**

The average American pays more in taxes than is often suspected. Because taxes are levied in so many different and often disguised ways, most workers have only a vague conception of how taxes affect their family budget. It turns out, however, that the National Taxpayers' Union has already made these calculations for us. The NTU figures that the total tax burden on a family with a median income of $52,895 in 1991 was $26,689—an incredible 50.4 percent of earnings. In other words, the government takes home a larger share than the worker. (See Figure 4-1). Here's where all the money goes:

```
Median Family Income ............................................$52,895
Federal income taxes................................................(5,585)
Social Security employee share...............................(3,774)
Social Security employer share ...............................(3,774)
Gasoline and other excise taxes..................................(123)
State/local sales taxes ...............................................(1,148)
State/local income taxes ...........................................(2,063)
Share of corporate income..........................................(328)
Taxes on production of goods and services..............(7,911)
Other taxes...............................................................(1,983)

The government's share ...........................................$26,689
The family's share .....................................................$26,206
```

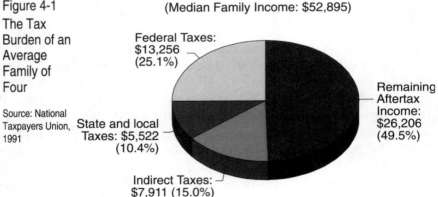

Figure 4-1
The Tax Burden of an Average Family of Four

Source: National Taxpayers Union, 1991

(Median Family Income: $52,895)

Federal Taxes: $13,256 (25.1%)

State and local Taxes: $5,522 (10.4%)

Indirect Taxes: $7,911 (15.0%)

Remaining Aftertax Income: $26,206 (49.5%)

An even handier way of calculating the true tax burden on middle income workers is to measure how much pre-tax income workers must earn to be able to purchase the products and services they want.

Take this example: How much money does a middle-income worker have to earn to be able to purchase a new car with a sticker price of $10,000?

## Feeding the Beast

When they calculate the cost of the car, most people forget to factor in the taxes paid on the income that is used to pay for the car. That is, *they forget to account for the federal income tax, the state income tax, and the federal payroll taxes that the tax collector takes straight off the top of our paychecks.*

Let's assume that our worker is a self-employed woman earning $40,000 a year and living in Michigan—an average tax state. She must earn $18,320 to buy the $10,000 car. Here's why. First, she must pay a $400 Michigan sales tax, which raises the retail price to $10,400. But to earn $10,400 in take-home pay, she must earn $18,320 in salary from which are deducted: $784 in Michigan income tax, $2,589 in self-employment (FICA taxes), and $4,551 in federal income tax.

To put it another way, the wage earner must work about three months to pay for the car and about two-and-a-half months just to pay the taxes on the income to purchase it. Here is the breakdown of these taxes.

Taxes:
State sales tax ................................................................. $400
State income tax ............................................................. 784
FICA payroll tax ............................................................... 1,303
Federal income tax ......................................................... 4,551
Total taxes ....................................................................... $7,038

Earnings required to purchase car:
Wage earner .................................................................... $17,038
Self-employed worker ..................................................... $18,320
(Extra self-employment tax of $1,286)

Source: Steve Moore and George Nastas, *Consumers Guide to Taxes*, Cato Institute, 1992

But it gets worse. Suppose our self-employed worker is unlucky enough to live in one of the high-tax states, such as California or New York. The true price of the car after accounting for sales taxes, income taxes, and self-employment taxes rises to as much as $20,186. More than half the income used to pay for the car is swallowed up in taxes. And this analysis does not even include the taxes paid by the car manufacturer, which raised the price of the car.

## ◆ The Tax Bite Over Time

As the above examples illustrate, when combining federal, state, and local taxes, many middle-income Americans spend a larger share of their workday working for Uncle Sam than for themselves or their families. It was not always thus. Figure 4-2 shows the percentage of national income that has been seized by government in taxes since the beginning of the century:

- In 1900 workers paid one of every ten income dollars in taxes.
- In 1930 workers paid one of every nine income dollars in taxes.
- In 1950 workers paid one of every four income dollars in taxes.
- In 1994 workers paid well over one of every three income dollars in taxes. For many workers, the taxman collects one of every two dollars of income.

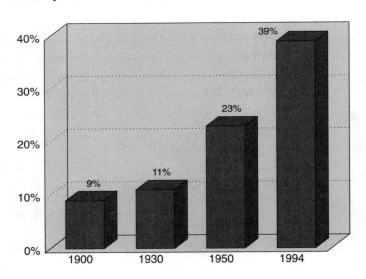

Figure 4-2
Federal, State and Local Taxes as a Share of National Income

Source: *Facts and Figures on Government Finance*, various years; and Tax Foundation, *Tax Features*.

The Tax Foundation calculates that government in America now collects $2 trillion a year. This tax burden is most easily understood by expressing it on a per-household basis, as shown in Figure 4-3.

- In 1900 the average family paid $1,370 in taxes.
- In 1950 the average family paid $6,970 in taxes.
- In 1994 the average family paid $18,600 in taxes.

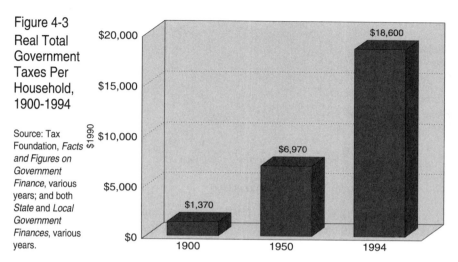

Figure 4-3
Real Total Government Taxes Per Household, 1900-1994

Source: Tax Foundation, *Facts and Figures on Government Finance*, various years; and both *State* and *Local Government Finances*, various years.

Taxes are now the largest expenditure in the family budget, according to the Tax Foundation. For a middle income family, taxes now consume more of the household budget than food, clothing, transportation, education, insurance, pensions, and recreation *combined*. No wonder more and more Americans doubt they are getting their money's worth from government.

## ◆ Washington's Tax Tale

In his first inaugural address, Jefferson urged that "a wise and frugal government, which shall restrain men from injuring one another ... shall not take from the mouth of labor the bread it has earned."

As Figure 4-4 shows, for the first 100 years of the nation, the Jeffersonian philosophy of limited taxation mostly prevailed. By 1900 the per capita federal tax burden was still only $110—compared to $4,000 today. The limited source of revenues for the federal government was a natural and intentional restraint on its expenditures. The three events that changed that were the imposition of the income tax in 1913, the two World Wars, and the creation of the Social Security program with its payroll taxes.

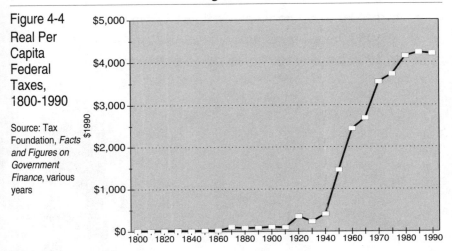

Figure 4-4 Real Per Capita Federal Taxes, 1800-1990

Source: Tax Foundation, *Facts and Figures on Government Finance*, various years

### ◆ The Income Tax Monstrosity

Until the ratification of the 16th Amendment in 1913, the court had consistently ruled the income tax unconstitutional. No law has contributed more to the growth of government than the federal income tax.

Even at the time of its passage, the income tax was a highly controversial measure. Most opinion leaders at around the turn of the century recognized the boundless potential for evil that the income tax represented. Here are what some of the critics said:

> "A vicious, inequitable, unpopular, impolitic, and socialistic act," complained The New York Times *of the first income tax to pass Congress in 1894. It went on to say that the tax was* "the most unreasoning and un-American movement in the politics of the last quarter-century."

> "It is an abhorrent and calamitous monstrosity," wrote The Washington Post *of the idea of a graduated income tax in that same year.* "It punishes everyone who rises above the rank of mediocrity. The fewer additional yokes put around the necks of the people, the better."

*"When men get in the habit of helping themselves to the property of others, they cannot be easily cured of it,"* insisted another New York Times *editorial slamming the proposed Constitutional amendment legitimizing the income tax in 1909.*

The income tax was eventually ratified because its supporters promoted it as a levy that would fall *only on the wealthiest Americans* while exempting the middle class from the pain. Rep. Cordell Hull, who drafted the first income tax, argued that its purpose was to force "the Carnegies, the Vanderbilts, the Morgans, and the Rockefellers with their aggregated billions of hoarded wealth" to pay a *fair share* of the tax burden.

Critics of the first income tax also claimed that it would not be long before the rates were raised to the unthinkable level of 10 percent. Supporters assured a skeptical public that such critics were mindless scaremongers. Yet as Figure 4-5 shows:

- In 1916 the top rate more than doubled to 16 percent.
- In 1917, the start of World War I, the rate was raised to 67 percent.
- In 1944, during World War II, the rate was raised to 94 percent. In other words, the government took 94 cents of every additional dollar earned and the worker kept 6 cents.

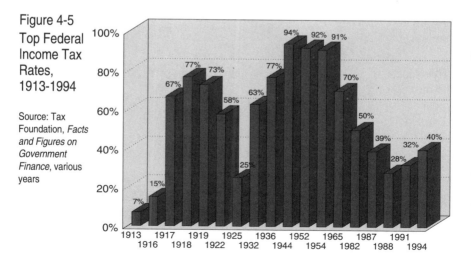

Figure 4-5
Top Federal Income Tax Rates, 1913-1994

Source: Tax Foundation, *Facts and Figures on Government Finance*, various years

- In the 1950s the tax rate remained at 91 percent.
- During the Reagan years the top marginal rate fell to 28 percent.
- President Clinton recently raised the top marginal tax rate to 40 percent.

One consistent pattern that has emerged over the past 75 years is that each time the income tax has been raised during wartime, Congress has neglected to return tax rates to their pre-war levels once the fighting has ended.

Congress has also always used progressive "soak the rich" rhetoric as a ruse to get the proverbial camel's nose under the tent so that middle class taxes can eventually be raised. After World War I, which was the first time that the income tax became a broad-based levy, the income tax was now recognized by politicians as a singularly powerful cash generator.

The secret of the income tax, however, is that it has never been "the rich man's tax." Congress has gathered added revenues from the income tax only by imposing a larger share onto the backs of the middle class. This has been achieved by gradually increasing the number of taxpayers required to file income tax returns and by raising not so much the *marginal* tax rates on the rich, but the *average* tax rates on the middle class. Although only two percent of the wealthiest families paid this tax in 1913, by the end of World War II virtually all families had to file. In 1914, 358,000 returns were filed; today

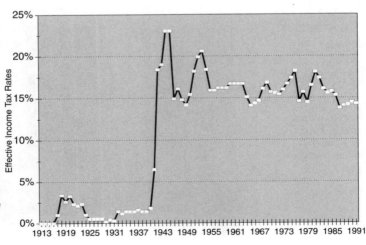

Figure 4-6 Effective Income Tax Rates for a Family of Four Earning $50,000

Source: Barro and Sahasakul, quoted in Bruce Bartlett, *The Futility of Raising Tax Rates*, Cato Institute, 1993.

## Feeding the Beast

there are over 100 million filed. That's a 30,000 fold increase in the number of people required to file returns over a time when the U.S. population rose by just 150 percent.

Figure 4-6 documents the steady rise in the effective tax rate that this expanding pool of workers has been forced to pay. The effective rate on a family with an income of $50,000 (in 1990 dollars) was never more than four percent until World War II. Since then it has been consistently above 14 percent. Similarly, the marginal tax rate on the middle class never rose above eight percent prior to World War II. Since then, it has never fallen below 22 percent and reached as high as 33 percent during the high-inflation, bracket-creep years of the 1980s.

There is little question that the income tax has served as a powerful engine of government growth in this century. Here are some numbers that confirm this: The *original* income tax raised less than $50 billion in 1990 dollars. Today the federal government raises about $700 billion from the income tax (corporate and personal). Figure 4-7 shows the increase over time. The first income tax amounted to about $50 per family (1990 dollars), whereas today the per household income tax burden is over $5,000.

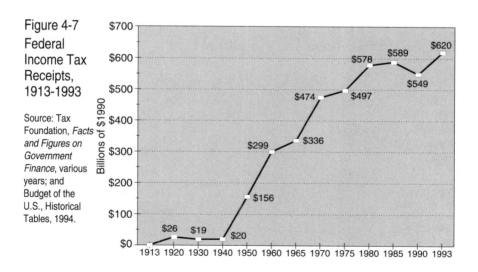

Figure 4-7
Federal Income Tax Receipts, 1913-1993

Source: Tax Foundation, *Facts and Figures on Government Finance*, various years; and Budget of the U.S., Historical Tables, 1994.

*Feeding the Beast*

### ◆ Convoluted and Complicated Compliance Costs

One way to measure the increased complexity of the income tax code since its inception is to examine the mountain of forms and paperwork that it now requires. The original 1040 form was four pages in all—and that included the instruction booklet, which *The New York Times* printed in its entirety on a single newspaper page. Now there are more than 4,000 pages of forms and instructions.

Even worse, consider the pages of federal law required to explain the legal nuances of the Internal Revenue code. (See Figure 4-8.)

- In the 1913 income tax there were 14 pages of federal law.
- By 1954 there were 984 pages of federal law on the income tax.
- By 1985 there were 3,975 pages of federal law on the income tax.
- By 1992 there were over 9,400 pages of federal law on the income tax.

What is most distressing about this surge in the complexity of the tax code is that in 1986 we passed a tax reform bill that was supposed to represent tax "simplification"!

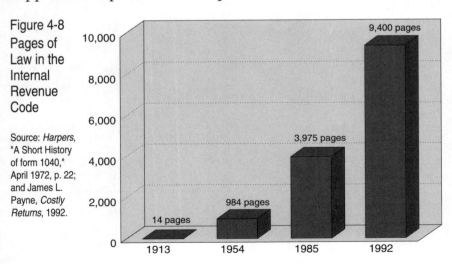

Figure 4-8
Pages of Law in the Internal Revenue Code

Source: *Harpers*, "A Short History of form 1040," April 1972, p. 22; and James L. Payne, *Costly Returns*, 1992.

## Feeding the Beast

According to official estimates, in 1985 American workers and businesses spent more than five billion man-hours computing their taxes, as documented below. This is more man-hours than are used to build every car, van, and truck in the United States in a given year, and represents a deadweight loss to the economy of more than $250 billion. (Remember the income tax only collects about $700 billion in revenue a year.) All of this complexity is music to the ears of attorneys and tax accountants. It is very maddening and costly for the rest of us.

**Individual Taxpayers:**
| | |
|---|---|
| Record keeping | 783 |
| Learning about tax requirements | 313 |
| Preparation | 553 |
| Copying and sending forms | 164 |
| Subtotal | 1,813 million man-hours |

**Business Taxpayers:**
| | |
|---|---|
| Record keeping | 1,957 |
| Learning about tax requirements | 196 |
| Obtaining materials | 133 |
| Locating and using preparer | 207 |
| Preparation | 1,034 |
| Copying and sending forms | 86 |
| Subtotal | 3,614 million man-hours |

**Total** ..... 5,427 million man-hours

Source: Arthur D. Little, Inc. *Development of Methodology for Estimating the Taxpayer Paperwork Burden* (Washington, D.C.: Internal Revenue Service, June 1988), p. I-7, Table I-1; and James L. Payne, *Costly Returns*, 1992. Note: Totals do not add because of rounding.

*Feeding the Beast*

Increasingly the income tax has moved away from the honor system. There are more and more IRS auditors and agents snooping into our business and personal affairs. See Figure 4-9.

- In 1913 the IRS had 4,000 employees.
- In 1973 the IRS had 82,000 employees.
- in 1993 the IRS had 125,000 employees.

Congress keeps appropriating more and more money for the tax collectors to do their snooping. In 1913 the first IRS budget was $80 million. Adjusted for inflation, today it is over $5.0 billion.

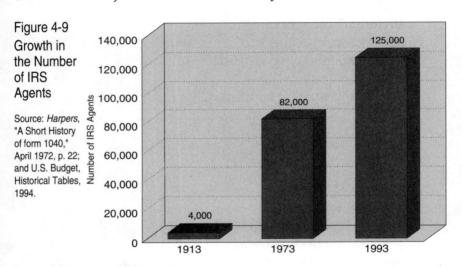

Figure 4-9
Growth in the Number of IRS Agents

Source: *Harpers*, "A Short History of form 1040," April 1972, p. 22; and U.S. Budget, Historical Tables, 1994.

### ◆ Taxing Families First

Thanks to the rising tide of federal taxes, raising a family in the United States in the 1990s is becoming unaffordable. Take a typical middle-income family of four: Jack, Dianne, little Billy, and little Susy. In the 1950s, Dianne probably worked at home taking care of the kids, while Jack supported the family on a single income. Jack paid only about four percent of his income in taxes to Uncle Sam. Most of the rest was take-home pay.

These days, the situation is entirely different. If they are like many modern couples, Jack and Dianne probably both work—Dianne perhaps less than full time. Jack and Dianne pay roughly 24 percent of their combined income in federal taxes.

Studies show that parents like Jack and Dianne spend about 20 percent less time with their kids today than forty years ago.

Why so much less family time? Parents have to be out working more, in large part because taxes on families with children are so much higher—see Figure 4-10.

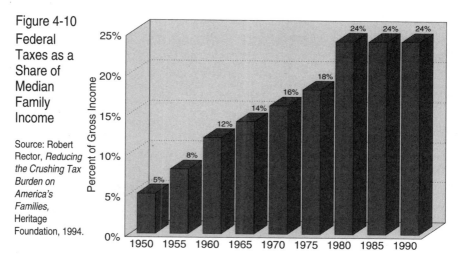

Figure 4-10
Federal Taxes as a Share of Median Family Income

Source: Robert Rector, *Reducing the Crushing Tax Burden on America's Families*, Heritage Foundation, 1994.

The major reason for this heftier tax burden on families with children is that the tax exemption for children has been eroded by inflation.

- In 1948 the dependent exemption was worth 42 percent of average family income, but that fell to 16 percent in 1970, and is just 12 percent today.
- The failure of the personal exemption to keep pace with inflation means that a family with four children pays about $5,000 more in taxes in 1994 than it would have in 1948.

## ◆ The Job Destruction Tax

Another oft-overlooked reason why middle class families are feeling such a financial pinch these days is that Social Security payroll taxes have continually risen since their inception in 1937. Figure 4-11 shows:

- The first Social Security payroll tax rate, which was in place from 1937 to 1950, was two percent.
- By 1970, after the introduction of Medicare and the hospital insurance tax, that rate was up to 9.6 percent.

- By 1980 the Social Security payroll tax rate was up to 12.3 percent.
- By 1990 the Social Security payroll tax rate was up to 15.3 percent.

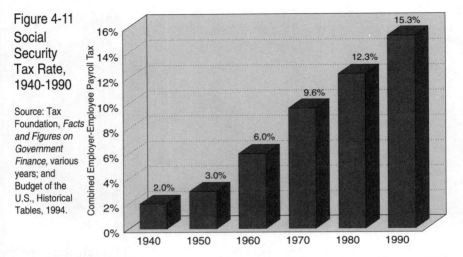

Figure 4-11
Social Security Tax Rate, 1940-1990

Source: Tax Foundation, *Facts and Figures on Government Finance*, various years; and Budget of the U.S., Historical Tables, 1994.

Today, a family with an income of $35,000 pays roughly $5,250 in Social Security payroll taxes. But for the politicians in Washington, this isn't nearly enough. Even with a 15 percent payroll tax rate, Social Security and Medicare are going bankrupt.

### ◆ High Taxes Stymie Economic Growth

Perhaps the largest indirect cost of government in America is the huge economic drain of our tax system. In the United States, we discourage work and employment through the income and payroll taxes, we discourage investment and savings through the personal and corporate income taxes, and we discourage entrepreneurial activity—which is the ultimate source of jobs—through the capital gains tax.

Taxes also harm our economy in that marginal tax rates on labor and capital are higher than necessary to raise the revenue needed to run the government (even at today's gigantic size). Because high marginal tax rates undermine business activity, output is some $410 billion lower than under a more economically efficient tax system. That is, if we had a flatter tax rate, the job-destroying and work onerous effects of taxes would be far lower than they are under current law.

Economic output would be about ten percent higher today than it is, if we had a more sensible tax system. (See Figure 4-12). Or to put it another way, the average family in the U.S. would be $5,000 richer today if America had reduced tax rates and taxes on capital years ago.

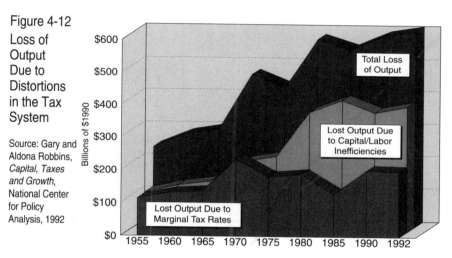

Figure 4-12
Loss of Output Due to Distortions in the Tax System

Source: Gary and Aldona Robbins, *Capital, Taxes and Growth*, National Center for Policy Analysis, 1992

Other economists confirm the validity of this finding. For example, Harvard economist Dale Jorgenson calculates a very large loss of potential economic output due to tax distortions. He finds that every dollar of taxes raised by the federal government today costs the economy about 18 cents. That translates into roughly a $200 billion per year loss in GNP. Jorgenson warns that further tax increases will carry even heavier distortions. Every additional dollar of taxes raised now costs the economy almost 40 cents. The Clinton 1993 tax hike, for example, can be expected to reduce national output over five years by a total of nearly $100 billion. This is equivalent to the reduction of pre-tax income of about $1,000 per family.

*Feeding the Beast*

### ◆ The State and Local Tax Burden

Taxes on the state level have in the past several decades run parallel to federal taxes. State revenues as a share of income have almost doubled since 1960, rising from 4.9 percent of GDP then, to 8.6 percent today (See Figure 4-13). There's no sign that the bleeding is slowing. 1990 and 1991 were the two largest tax increase years in the history of state government.

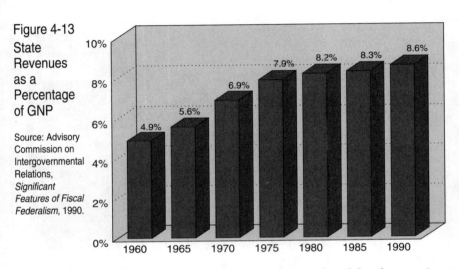

Figure 4-13
State Revenues as a Percentage of GNP

Source: Advisory Commission on Intergovernmental Relations, *Significant Features of Fiscal Federalism*, 1990.

States have also followed Uncle Sam's lead by becoming much more dependent upon income taxes as a source of revenues in the past fifty years. Prior to World War II only a handful of states imposed any income tax. Today, only nine states do not have an income tax, and four of those are considering introducing one. Today state and local governments raise about $120 billion per year through income taxes. Figure 4-14 shows the rising share of income taxes as a percentage of total state and local taxes.

- ◆ In 1900 state and local governments raised none of their revenues through income taxes.
- ◆ In 1960 state and local governments raised 10 percent of their revenues through income taxes.
- ◆ In 1992 state and local governments raised 27 percent of their revenues through income taxes.

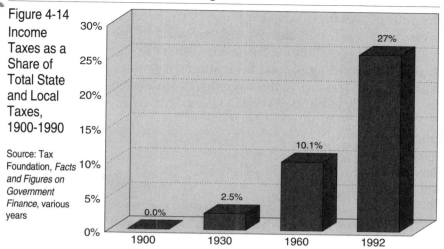

Figure 4-14 Income Taxes as a Share of Total State and Local Taxes, 1900-1990

Source: Tax Foundation, *Facts and Figures on Government Finance*, various years

In the 1980s, one thousand people each and every day fled the 10 highest income tax states for the 10 lowest income tax states. Nearly 4 million people voted with their feet in favor of low income taxes.

### ♦ The Truth About the Reagan Tax Cuts

Many Americans are mystified as to how federal taxes can be so high today? After all, didn't Ronald Reagan pass a massive income tax cut in 1981? The answer is yes, but. Yes, Reagan did sign a 25 percent income tax rate cut for all Americans in 1981. But what the right hand of Congress gave in 1981, the left hand of Congress took away from 1982-1993. There have been six major tax increases—1982, 1983, 1984, 1987, 1988, 1990, and 1993—since. These have essentially canceled the Reagan tax cuts.

The whole experience of the Reagan tax cuts has been so thoroughly misrepresented that the mythology of the era has supplanted the reality. This kind of historical revisionism is lethal. As the saying goes: "Those who fail to learn the lessons of history are doomed to repeat them." So let's learn the real fiscal lessons of the 1980s and dismiss the fairy tales.

*The Reagan tax cuts did not cause the budget deficits of the 1980s.* This is the ultimate distortion about the 1980s. Here's why: From 1980 through 1990 federal tax receipts in current dollars doubled from $517 billion to $1 trillion as shown in Figure 4-15. This was a seven percent annual growth rate in tax revenues, or almost twice

*Feeding the Beast*

the rate of inflation. The problem is that federal outlays grew even faster. As David Rosenbaum reported in the *New York Times* in 1992: "One popular misconception is that the Republican tax cuts caused the crippling federal budget deficit now approaching $300 billion a year. The fact is, the large deficit resulted because the government vastly expanded what it spent each year . . . ."

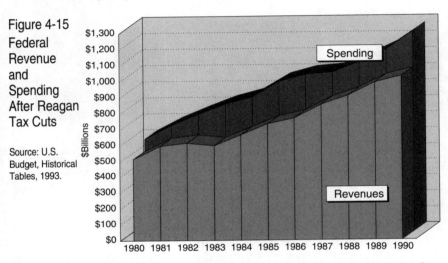

Figure 4-15
Federal Revenue and Spending After Reagan Tax Cuts

Source: U.S. Budget, Historical Tables, 1993.

The other popular myth about the Reagan tax cuts is that they were a huge tax cut for the rich. Rep. Richard Gephardt recently stated this conventional line that has almost become part of our culture: "For the last ten years we have warned of a day of reckoning resulting from tax cuts for the rich and neglect of the middle class." The problem with this reasoning is that in the 1980s the rich paid both *more* taxes in total dollars and a larger share of the total tax burden. Figure 4-16 shows:

- The share of the total tax burden paid by the richest one percent of taxpayers rose from 18 percent in 1981 to 25 percent in 1990.
- Taxes paid by the richest five percent rose from 35 percent of the total to 44 percent of the total.
- The share of taxes paid by lower 50 percent of taxpayers fell from seven to six percent.

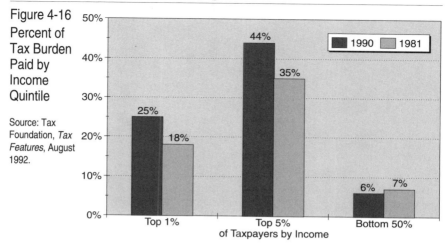

Figure 4-16
Percent of Tax Burden Paid by Income Quintile

Source: Tax Foundation, *Tax Features*, August 1992.

### ◆ Conclusion

In the famous Supreme Court case *McCulloch v. Maryland*, Chief Justice Marshall wrote: "The power to tax involves the power to destroy." Are we allowing taxes to destroy our country? Two trillion dollars is an awesome amount of money to expropriate from businesses and workers and families to pay for a government that doesn't work very well. The real tragedy is that even after taking in all of this cash, the government has still managed to find itself up to its eyeballs in debt.

Exit polls taken during the 1992 election asked the question: "Would you prefer fewer government services and lower taxes, or more government services and higher taxes?" By a 55 to 36 percent margin, voters said they wanted less government services and lower taxes.

### Recommended Reading

Lindsey, Larry, *The Growth Experiment*. Basic Books, 1990

Payne, James L. *Costly Returns: The Burden of the U.S. Tax System*. ICS Press, 1991

# 5

# The Regulatory Stranglehold

> *It will be of little avail to the people that the laws are made by men of their own choice if the laws be so voluminous that they cannot be read, or so incoherent that they cannot be understood.*
> -The Federalist Papers

In recent decades the political establishment in Washington has sought out additional methods of asserting command over the nation's activities. An estimated 10 to 20 percent of national output above and beyond what is consumed in taxes and spending is now effectively controlled by government regulators. Economists estimate that about 30 percent of the decline in manufacturing wages since the early 1970s is due to regulations passed by the EPA and OSHA alone.

In just the last several years there has been a proliferation of federal regulations. These costly rules are stealth tax hikes imposed on U.S. consumers and businesses. Ultimately, they make America poorer.

## ◆ The Fourth Branch of Government

The U.S. Constitution says that we are *supposed* to have three branches of government; but, in fact, we have four. Regulatory agencies today serve as an extra-Constitutional, independent, and non-elected fourth branch of government.

## The Regulatory Stranglehold

Some regulations, of course, have a positive impact on our lives. Some regulations make sense; others don't—yet there is no process on the federal level for sorting out the sensible regulations from the senseless ones.

One inexact way of measuring the government regulatory burden is by adding up the pages of regulations in the Federal Register. Using this measure as an index, Figure 5-1 shows how regulations have grown each decade since 1940. If we examine the ebb and flow of regulation over the past 60 years, we see:

- In 1935 there were 4,000 pages in the Federal Register.
- In 1950 there were 12,000 pages in the Federal Register.
- In 1980 the number of pages in the Federal Register peaked at 87,000 under Jimmy Carter.
- Ronald Reagan's anti-regulation policies reduced regulations to 48,000 pages in 1985.
- Under George Bush regulations climbed back to 65,000 pages in 1990.
- After Bill Clinton's first year in office, regulations climbed to more than 70,000.
- If this trend continues by 1995 the number of pages in the Federal Register will hit an all time high of 90,000.

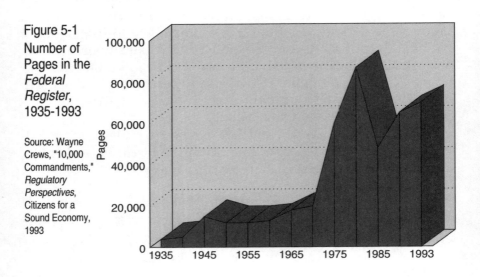

Figure 5-1
Number of Pages in the *Federal Register*, 1935-1993

Source: Wayne Crews, "10,000 Commandments," *Regulatory Perspectives*, Citizens for a Sound Economy, 1993

## The Regulatory Stranglehold

If you stacked one copy of each of the Federal Registers from the past twelve years on top of each other, you could build a tower that would rise to the height of the Washington Monument. And keep in mind that these are just the generic regulations. There are tens of thousands of added regulations to inform businesses how to conform with the government's rules.

Figure 5-2 shows the increase in the number of new labor laws since 1945 as compiled by the Washington D.C.-based Labor Policy Institute:

- By 1950 there were 3 new labor laws enacted.
- By 1970 there were 19 new labor laws enacted.
- By 1991 there were 90 new labor laws enacted.

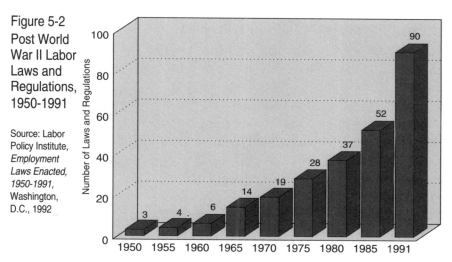

Figure 5-2
Post World War II Labor Laws and Regulations, 1950-1991

Source: Labor Policy Institute, *Employment Laws Enacted, 1950-1991*, Washington, D.C., 1992

Regulation has exploded in the area of labor law. Labor regulations are often well-meaning mandates on business to provide benefits and protections to workers. But they often carry a heavy price tag in lost jobs and higher consumer costs. For example, the 1989 minimum wage increase contributed to a record high 24 percent teenage unemployment rate in 1992.

Surveys suggest that most workers would rather have more pay and less parental and sick leave, if they could choose between the two. But the government now mandates that employers provide more parental leave than the employees would otherwise choose—and thus less cash salary. Yet the politicians who vote for such laws, can boast of their beneficence toward the very working men and women they have, in fact, harmed.

Social and economic regulation has run much the same course. In the entire nineteenth century the U.S. Congress passed 14 social and economic regulatory laws. In just the ten years of the 1970s the government passed 125 such laws.

Another method of calculating the impact of regulation on the economy over time is to examine the regulatory apparatus of the Washington agencies that enforce both social and economic regulation. In 1900 there were 10 regulatory agencies, today there are 52. Figure 5-3 shows that from 1970 to 1992 the budgets of federal regulatory agencies have ballooned by nearly 200 percent. Over this same time period the number of federal regulators nearly doubled, from 70,000 to 130,000 [Figure 5-4].

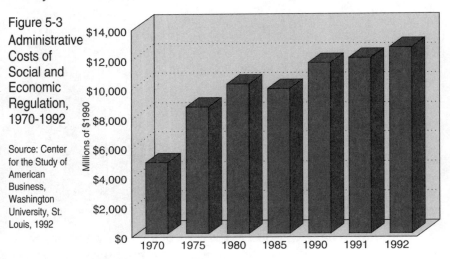

Figure 5-3
Administrative Costs of Social and Economic Regulation, 1970-1992

Source: Center for the Study of American Business, Washington University, St. Louis, 1992

### ◆ The Buck Doesn't Stop Here

Increasingly, Washington is shifting costly new activities onto the backs of state and local governments. Federal mandates are a growing cost of doing business for local government all over the country:

- ◆ The town of Anchorage, Alaska calculates that federal mandates cost the city over $500 per homeowner.
- ◆ Lewiston, Maine says that federal mandates cost city hall over $600 per household. That's almost half the city budget.

## The Regulatory Stranglehold

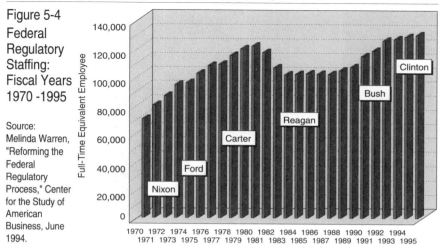

Figure 5-4 Federal Regulatory Staffing: Fiscal Years 1970-1995

Source: Melinda Warren, "Reforming the Federal Regulatory Process," Center for the Study of American Business, June 1994.

♦ The U.S. General Accounting Office estimates that federal mandates now cost states and localities as much as $500 billion a year.

Figure 5-5 shows that these federal mandates and spending requirements are a relatively recent phenomenon. From 1930 through 1960 Congress passed just two of these laws. From 1960 to 1990 Congress passed more than 70. In 1991 there were nearly 500 proposed new regulations before Congress that would affect states and localities.

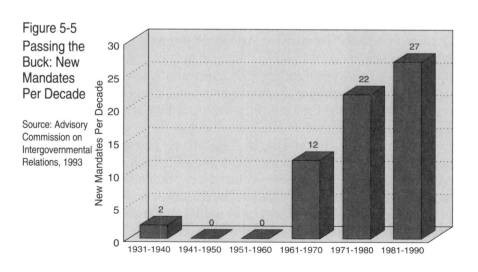

Figure 5-5 Passing the Buck: New Mandates Per Decade

Source: Advisory Commission on Intergovernmental Relations, 1993

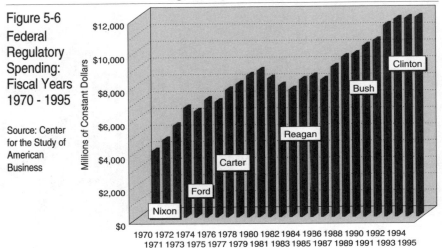

Figure 5-6
Federal Regulatory Spending: Fiscal Years 1970 - 1995

Source: Center for the Study of American Business

Congress has proven that it can't balance the federal budget, and it appears determined to ensure that states and cities can't balance theirs, either.

◆ **Regulatory Overkill**

As the regulatory apparatus in Washington has proliferated, so too have the compliance costs imposed on American workers, businesses, and consumers. For example, the Clean Air Act Amendments passed in 1990 were well-intended. We all want clean air and a pristine environment. But whereas the benefits of that law are expected to amount to about $14 billion per year, the costs are expected to exceed $30 billion. The law could lower America's GNP by almost one-half percentage point—every year, forever.

It is a huge undertaking to determine how much regulatory overkill drains from our economy. Estimates range from $300 billion to $1.7 trillion. But the only fair way to assess the price tag of *bad* government, is to offset the costs versus the economic, environmental and social benefits of regulation. The issue here is: Do government edicts produce these benefits in a cost-minimizing manner and without undue burden on businesses, workers, and consumers? Another way to ask the question is: Are there cheaper ways to yield the same level of benefit? The answer is almost certainly *yes*. To cite several examples:

## *The Regulatory Stranglehold*

- Acid rain prevention laws require that coal, steel and other industries spend hundreds of millions of dollars on anti-pollution controls to protect rivers and lakes. Yet alternative techniques, such as the liming of lakes, would have a much more positive impact in preventing damage from acid rain at a fraction of the cost.

- The layers upon layers of Food and Drug Administration regulations of newly developed drugs and vaccines needlessly delay the introduction of potentially life saving treatments for AIDs, muscular dystrophy, and other diseases. These delays of months and often years cause increased human suffering and death, higher drug prices, and less innovation.

- Minimum wage laws have sent black teenage unemployment rates to up to 40 percent in many areas.

Economists have concluded that a reasonable estimate for the net cost of regulation is about $400 billion per year. That is, society could have the same benefits that we *attempt to get* through regulation-clean air and water, healthy and mostly injury-free work places, safe products on the market, safeguards against discrimination, and so forth—and still save about $4,000 per household at the same time. That's more than three times the amount of money the federal government raises each year from the corporate income tax.

Figure 5-7
Number of Pages in Federal Register vs. S&P500/GNP

Sources: Marvin Zonis & Assoc.; U.S. Bureau of Economic Analysis; U.S. Bureau of the Census; Standard & Poor's Corp.

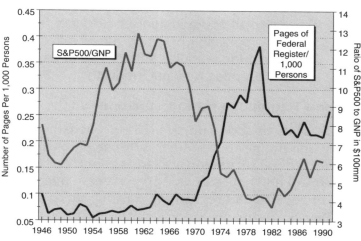

*The Regulatory Stranglehold*

### ◆ Good Intentions Run Amok

Almost all regulations passed by Congress have the noblest of intentions. After all, who is against preserving the environment and wildlife? Ensuring safe drinking water? Workplace safety? Protecting against unsafe foods and products? Safeguarding the rights and opportunities of the disabled and minorities?

Notwithstanding good intentions, the regulatory stranglehold is choking the life out of America's economic vitality as surely as any agent of deliberate malice. The reason is that what we have seen in America over the past thirty years is not so much a proliferation of regulation, as it is a proliferation of moronic and destructive regulation. Researchers at the Heritage Foundation recently calculated the human cost of some of our more absurd regulations. Heritage finds:

- ◆ It would cost $4.2 billion to save just one life under the hazardous waste disposal ban. With this money, 47,000 criminals could be kept in prison for three and a half years.
- ◆ It would cost $119 billion to avert just one death under the formaldehyde occupational exposure limit. With that much money, we could develop and bring to market 330 potentially life-saving new drugs.
- ◆ Instead of spending $92 billion to save one life under the atrazine/alachlor drinking water standard, cancer research at the National Institute of Health could be quadrupled for the next 12 years.
- ◆ The Office of Management and Budget estimates that one EPA regulation on wood preservatives would cost $5.7 trillion for every life saved. This is as much as the entire U.S. Gross National Product!

### ◆ How Regulation Harms Consumers

Regulations add as much as 33 percent to the cost of building an airplane engine and as much as 95 percent to the price of a new vaccine. Federal regulation also adds about $3,000 to the cost of a new car. All told, an estimated 80 percent of overall inflation is a result of government regulation, pushing up costs.

There is also an inverse relationship between the total number of government regulators and private sector job growth. [Figure 5-8]

## The Regulatory Stranglehold

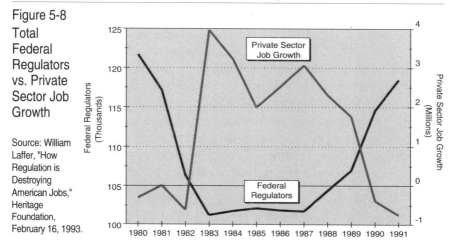

Figure 5-8
Total Federal Regulators vs. Private Sector Job Growth

Source: William Laffer, "How Regulation is Destroying American Jobs," Heritage Foundation, February 16, 1993.

### ◆ The Great Regulatory U-Turn

For a short while, Congress and the Presidency were actually succeeding in rolling back unnecessary regulation. From the late 1970s through the end of the 1980s, during the de-regulation era of Jimmy Carter and the anti-regulation era of Ronald Reagan, regulatory costs actually declined in real terms. But this progress was short-lived. In the 1990s we have returned to an era of heavy-fisted regulators inspired by a re-regulation Congress. As shown in Figure 5-9, regulatory costs peaked in 1977 at $540 billion, fell to less than $500 billion by the end of the 1980s, but

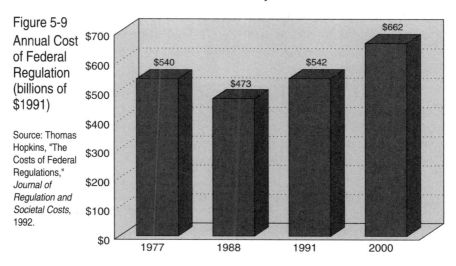

Figure 5-9
Annual Cost of Federal Regulation (billions of $1991)

Source: Thomas Hopkins, "The Costs of Federal Regulations," *Journal of Regulation and Societal Costs*, 1992.

now are expected to climb to a new peak of nearly $662 billion by 2000, according to scholar Thomas Hopkins of the Rochester Institute of Technology. Regulations now cost the average American household about $6,000 per year. When added to the cost of government spending, this means that the total burden of government is now about $30,000 per household.

The tragedy of this new era of regulation in the 1990s is that government failed to learn any important economic lessons from the benefits of deregulation. New empirical evidence documents the blessings of the de-regulation of the late 1970s and early 1980s.

- A new study by economist Charles Winston of the Brookings Institution calculates that the deregulation of seven industries—airlines, railroads, trucking, telecommunications, cable TV, brokerage firms, and natural gas—yielded $40 billion in welfare gains to U.S. consumers and businesses by 1990. This was the equivalent of an eight percent gain in GNP.
- De-regulation of trucking has led to the creation of nearly 500,000 new trucking jobs and 30,000 new carriers.
- The average U.S. household pays 50 percent less for home heating since deregulation of oil and gas.
- Rail transportation has experienced 60 percent fewer train accidents since freight train deregulation.
- Airplane travel is roughly 20 percent cheaper today (adjusted for inflation) than in the mid-1970s, before deregulation of the airlines. The average family of four saves about $200 on a long distance flight thanks to deregulation.

Estimates are that further deregulation of this type could generate at least $20 billion of additional gains to the American consumer. Yet in Washington de-regulation is virtually a dirty word these days. We can almost certainly expect more, not less, harmful regulation over the next decade.

### Recommended Reading

Crandall, Robert, *Why is the Cost of Environmental Regulation So High?* CSAB, Paper No. 110, Washington University, Feb. 1992

# 6

# The Federal Octopus

> *He has erected a multitude of New Offices,*
> *and sent hither swarms of Officers to harass our*
> *people, and eat out their substance.*
> The Declaration of Independence

Today, there are 18 million Americans working for federal, state and local governments with a combined annual salary and benefit package of close to $40 billion a year. Figure 6-1 highlights the growth of total public payrolls since 1940.

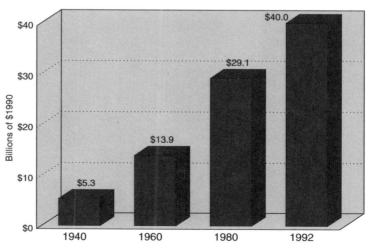

Figure 6-1
Total Government Monthly Payroll, 1940-1992

## The Federal Octopus

The 18 million people working for the government today is more than the number of people living in all the Northwestern states—Idaho, Montana, North Dakota, Oregon, South Dakota, Utah, Washington, Wyoming, and Nevada—combined. Even adjusting for population growth, the public payrolls have roughly tripled over this century, as shown in Figure 6-2.

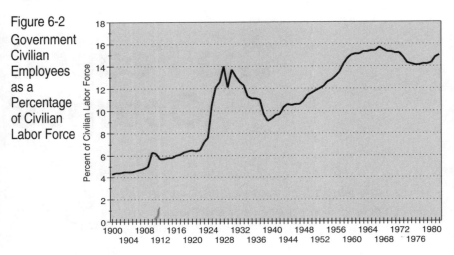

Figure 6-2
Government Civilian Employees as a Percentage of Civilian Labor Force

Still, over the past half-century, public employment has been one of America's fastest growing occupations. In fact, in 1992, for the first time in the nation's history, the government employed more workers than the entire manufacturing sector (See Figure 6-3). The regulators are beginning to outnumber the regulated.

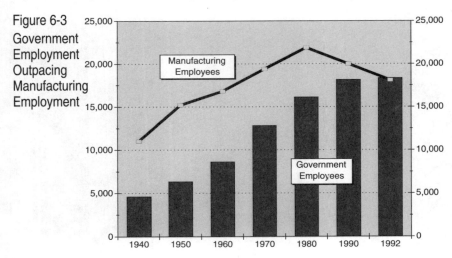

Figure 6-3
Government Employment Outpacing Manufacturing Employment

## The Federal Octopus

Figure 6-4
Where Unionization is Growing: Private vs. Public Sector Union Membership

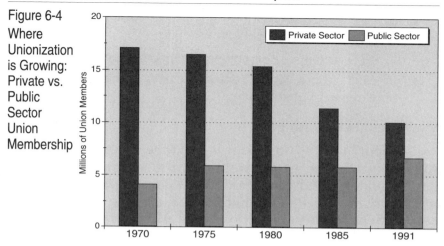

Because of changes in the U.S. workforce, union membership has been steadily shrinking over the past quarter-century in virtually every occupation except one: Government employment. Figure 6-4 contrasts the shrinkage of private sector union members with the explosion of public-sector union membership. Since 1970 unions have lost seven million private sector members, but over the same period, they added more than 2.5 million government employees to the rank and file. The obvious implication is that government employees compose an ever-rising share of union membership, as shown Figure 6-5.

Figure 6-5
Public Sector Share of Union Membership

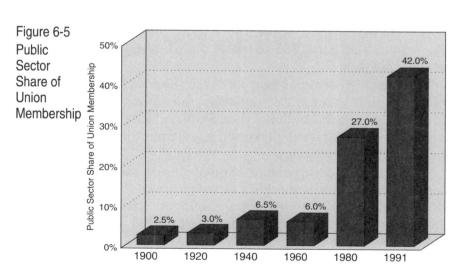

- In 1900, 2.5 percent of all union members were public employees.
- In 1960, about six percent were public employees.
- In 1991, about 42 percent of all union members were employees of government.

◆ **Welcome to Club Fed**

A report by the American Legislative Exchange Council (ALEC) finds that "average state and local government employee compensation (including wages, salaries, and employee benefits) has been rising much more quickly than average private sector compensation for 40 years." Specifically, ALEC reports:

- For every dollar of additional private sector compensation in the 1980s, government salaries and benefits soared by $6.32.
- In Michigan, real private sector pay declined by one percent in the 1980s, but local employee pay rose seven percent and state employee pay 16 percent.
- In Ohio, real private sector salaries dropped by two percent, but state pay grew by 20 percent.
- In Connecticut, real private sector pay rose by a healthy 16.5 percent. But that was trivial compared to the 53 percent real pay hike for state government employees in Hartford.
- In Washington state, the typical state government employee earns $250 a month more than a typical private employee.

If state and local pay had just kept pace with the growth in state personal income in the 1980s, the savings to taxpayers would have been $61 billion a year. State and local taxes could on average be reduced by 15 percent if it were not for excessive state and local government pay.

Side-by-side comparisons of government and private sector workers who do the same kind of work reveal that government is invariably the more generous employer—particularly when government benefits and job security are added into the calculation. Consider the following examples:

## The Federal Octopus

- The average public sector bus driver earns 70 percent more than the average private bus driver.
- Postal workers make fully one-third higher salaries and benefits than comparably skilled private sector workers. A former Postal Rate Commissioner recently complained that in many small towns in America, postal employees are the best paid workers in town.
- The voluntary quit rate from the federal government was lower in 1987 than the private sector quit rate during the depth of the Great Depression when unemployment rates exceeded 20 percent.
- Public school teachers out-earn teachers in the superior private schools by 54 percent on average.
- The *Washington Post* reports that one out of every ten residents of the District of Columbia is now on the city payroll.

One of the most bizarre stories about the lifestyles of our contemporary public servants involves a Philadelphia municipal employee who spent his afternoons playing pinball in a downtown bar while he was supposed to be on the job. The man was able to retain his $50,000 a year city job by convincing city officials that his pinball playing was a gambling addiction, and thus a disability.

### ◆ The Federal Octopus

Where does government put all these 18 million public employees? A clever and insightful 1930 essay, entitled "Federal Octopus"; remarked on the considerable similarities between the fertility of biological organisms and government agencies:

> *The bureau is, in the realm of government, what protozoa are in the realm of zoology. Originating as a single cell, they immediately begin to reproduce by fission, a self-division of the body into two or more complete cells. The protozoa abound in stagnant waters, as the bureau can flourish only in the stagnation of public spirit. Protozoa are parasites and the cause of certain diseases, as bureaus are parasitic and destructive of the vigor and health of the body politic. Again protozoa are the simplest and lowest form of animal life, just as bureau government is one of the earliest and crudest forms of arbitrary rule.*

## The Federal Octopus

> *Protozoa are apparently content to remain protozoa, but there the analogy ends; the bureau is ever striving onward and upward, and not only subdivides itself indefinitely, but each subdivision in turn seeks to elevate itself ultimately into a mighty department.*

Today this federal octopus has longer tentacles than ever before imagined. There is virtually a "mighty department" of government on every downtown street corner in Washington—each massive structure a monument to the growth of the government command and control economy.

Table 6-1 chronicles the creation of new federal cabinet agencies over the past two hundred years. The first Congress created just four cabinet agencies: The Department of State, the Department of War, the Department of the Navy, and the Treasury Department. Now there are sixteen. Remarkable as it may seem today, for the first fifty or so years of the nation, one single agency, the Treasury Department, handled all domestic affairs—which is

Table 6-1 Date of Founding of Cabinet Level Agencies

\* No longer in existence

\*\* Office of Attorney General established in 1789.

\*\*\* Department established in 1862, but did not become a cabinet-level agency until 1889.

| Department | Year Created |
|---|---|
| State (Foreign Affairs) | 1789 |
| Treasury | 1789 |
| Defense (War) | 1789 |
| Navy* | 1798 |
| Interior | 1849 |
| Justice** | 1870 |
| Agriculture*** | 1889 |
| Commerce and Labor* | 1903 |
| Commerce | 1913 |
| Labor | 1913 |
| Health, Education & Welfare* | 1953 |
| Housing and Urban Development | 1965 |
| Transportation | 1966 |
| Energy | 1977 |
| Health and Human Services | 1979 |
| Education | 1979 |
| Veterans Affairs | 1989 |

## The Federal Octopus

to say that it handled very little. In 1849 the Interior Department was founded and most domestic affairs, such as road building, were transferred to this agency.

Over the next one hundred years the federal government rapidly spawned new domestic cabinet agencies. The Justice Department was created in 1870; followed by the Agriculture Department in 1889; the Commerce Department in 1903; the Labor Department in 1913.

In the post-World War II period, congressional cabinet-making shifted into overdrive. The new agencies included:

- Health, Education and Welfare in 1953;
- Housing and Urban Development in 1965;
- Transportation in 1966;
- Energy in 1977;
- Education in 1979;
- Veterans Affairs in 1989.

Only two Cabinet Departments have been ended in the nation's history: The Department of the Navy and the Post Office, which was made an independent agency in 1970.

### ◆ The Washington Edifice Complex

The federal government is the primary owner of buildings in America—which is not surprising given that it has 18 million civilian workers to provide office space for.

- The federal government owns 450,000 buildings in the U.S. This is an increase of 30,000 since 1970.
- The federal government occupies 2.8 billion square feet of office and warehouse space—up from 2.5 billion in 1970.

The U.S. government is also the wealthiest landholder in the world. In fact, it is quite probable that wiping out the deficit and the entire national debt could be accomplished in one fell swoop by simply forcing the government to sell off its vast land holdings. These millions of acres are worth trillions of dollars—and that's not even counting the national treasures, such as the national parks.

Roughly one-third of all land area in the United States is owned by the federal government. It is estimated that at most half of this land has any environmental or recreational significance.

## The Federal Octopus

- The federal government owns 61 percent of Idaho.
- The federal government owns 79 percent of Nevada.
- The federal government owns 81 percent of Alaska.

The Department of the Interior owns 350,000 acres of land classified as "no longer needed for federal purposes." Some of this is urban land in areas such as Palm Springs, California. But what is truly unnerving is that the federal government spends nearly half a billion each year purchasing tens of thousands of additional acres.

### ◆ Awash in Lawyers

It is unlikely that any single occupation has prospered from the growth of government more than the legal profession. Public hostility toward attorneys has reached such heights that a joke book exclusively about lawyers recently made *The New York Times* best seller list. This public hostility is in many ways well-deserved. Anyway you measure it, America is overrun with lawyers. As James Davidson, chairman of the National Taxpayers Union, documents in his book *The Great Reckoning*:

- In 1990 America had more lawyers than the rest of the industrialized world combined.
- America has four times as many lawyers *per person* as Great Britain, five times as many as Germany, ten times as many as France, and almost twenty times more than Japan.
- The lawyer-surplus in America is so large that in a typical year there are more law school graduates from American universities than there are lawyers in Japan.

Figure 6-6 shows how the ratio of lawyers to population was relatively constant at about 1,200 per million residents from the time of the Civil War through World War II. But in the post-World War II era the legal profession has proliferated, with a near tripling of lawyers as a share of the population.

Washington contains twice as many lawyers per resident as other large U.S. cities and more lawyers than all of Japan.

The legal profession has a way of creating its own demand—particularly in Washington. For example, the 70,000 pages of rules and regulations published in the Federal Register are a monument to the growing political clout of the legal community. Thousands of six-figure salary government lawyers are needed

## The Federal Octopus

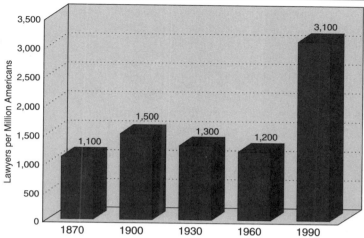

Figure 6-6 Number of Lawyers Per Million Americans, 1870-1990

to prepare this catalog of tedious legalese; then thousands more in private practice charging $150 - $200 an hour are needed to convert it all into standard English.

### ◆ The Litigation Explosion

What do America's lawyers do best? File lawsuits. The number of federal lawsuits nearly tripled from 1960 to 1990, which roughly parallels the growth in the number of lawyers. Although it is unclear which way the causality runs, there is no question that some percentage of these suits are frivolous and unproductive. Consider Superfund, an EPA program that was supposed to clean up toxic dumps, but which in reality has become a bountiful cash machine for clever lawyers and shady contractors. A study commissioned by Congress estimates that well over one-third of the $7.5 billion that has been spent by Superfund since the early 1980s has been swallowed up in legal and administrative costs.

The litigation crisis drives up the costs of everything—from automobiles to drugs. The following excerpt from a Wall Street Journal article underscores the economic lunacy of the legal system today:

> *Drunks and tort lawyers are surely toasting this week's award of $9 million to a visibly plastered Mexican dishwasher who stumbled in front of a New York subway train and woke up missing one arm. In awarding this jackpot, a Bronx jury heaped all blame on the Transit Authority for failing to "take charge" of the man.*

Researchers have begun to quantify a negative relationship between lawyering and economic growth. For example, professor Stephen Magee of the University of Texas analyzed 28 countries, comparing GNP growth with the percentage of lawyers in the work force. This highlights a simple relationship: More lawyers equal less growth. Magee calculates that each new law school graduate will reduce U.S. economic output by $2.5 million a year. Professor Magee reckons the nation has about 40 percent more lawyers than is economically healthy.

### ◆ The Costs of Litigation

These days it's not just defendants who are taken to the cleaners by the American legal system—America's global competitiveness suffers as well. Today the U.S. has more than 70 percent of the world's lawyers, who file more than 18 million lawsuits a year—an increasing number of them frivolous, but nonetheless hugely expensive. In 1992 the White House Council on Competitiveness issued a report concluding that "America is in the midst of a litigation explosion" and estimating that the cost of the litigation frenzy in America is as much as $300 billion in direct and indirect costs per year. At least 20 percent of these costs, or $60 billion a year, are avoidable.

Excessive litigation imposes negative effects on the economy in many ways, including:

- diversion of business time and effort to fighting off aggressive lawyers,
- overloaded court dockets and expensive delays,
- defensive medicine to prevent malpractice suits which contributes to spiraling health care costs,
- a reluctance to bring new products to market, and so forth.

The employee benefit consulting firm Lewin-VHI calculated in 1993 that defensive medicine to shield off lawsuits cost U.S. consumers from $36 billion to $78 billion annually.

Government liability and other legal reforms could take a huge chunk out of litigation-related costs by discouraging baseless lawsuits. These include "loser pay" rules which require the loser to pay the winner's legal costs (also known as the English

## The Federal Octopus

Rule), ceilings on awards for pain and suffering, and privatization of the court system by permitting and encouraging the use of alternative dispute resolution mechanisms.

### ◆ The Influence Peddlers

The only people who seemingly outnumber lawyers in Washington are lobbyists. The number of trade groups and consulting firms has grown so rapidly in the past four decades that there is now a group that lobbies for lobbyists! The Association of Associations now has a membership directory the size of a small phone book.

Congressional statistics document the steady rise of professional influence peddlers in Washington:

- ◆ In 1956 there were 4,900 national trade associations with a presence in Washington. Today there are 23,000.
- ◆ In 1960 there were 365 paid lobbyists of the Senate. Today, there are 40,100. In other words, there are more than 400 lobbyists for every Senator.
- ◆ In 1970 the American Association of Retired Persons (AARP) had two million members. In 1992 it had 34 million members. One in four registered voters, as AARP proudly claims, are members. And with a $300 million annual budget, it may be the single most vocal advocate for expanding the size of the state in America today. According to the National Taxpayers Union, AARP currently supports government programs and taxes that would cost taxpayers up to $1 trillion after ten years. That's almost $10,000 per household.

### ◆ PAC Attack

Political Action Committees (PACs) are one of Congress's most ingenious inventions of recent times. A PAC is a fund-raising arm of a special interest group created to raise money for political campaigns. The Teamsters Union, the AFL-CIO, the American Medical Association, and the realtors all give away $5 million-plus in presidential election years to candidates that support their causes. It is a wonderfully convenient *quid pro quo* for the special interest groups and their politicians.

## The Federal Octopus

First permitted in the early 1970s, the number of PACs has grown almost eight-fold in just two decades—from 608 to 4,700 in 1992. Real expenditures by PACS have grown even faster, as demonstrated by Figure 6-7.

- PACs spent $60 million in 1972.
- PACs spent $210 million in 1980.
- PACs spent $400 million in 1992.

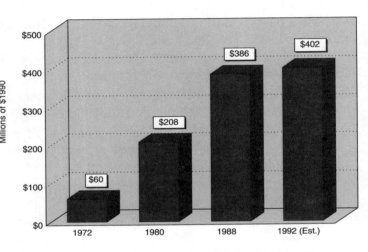

Figure 6-7
Campaign Contributions of Political Action Committees, 1972-1992

The first and only important rule of PACs is that they are almost all dedicated to the principle of protecting incumbents. For example, in 1988, for every dollar that PACs gave to a challenger, six dollars were funneled to a sitting member of Congress. PACs love incumbents—and the feeling is definitely mutual.

Why do we have such a massive predator economy in Washington? "All these lobbyists and lawyers did not get into business with the sworn aim of bleeding the country dry," remarks *National Journal* reporter Jonathan Rauch. "As with a bacillus or tapeworm, it's not that the parasite is evil; it's that it is just trying to get what it deserves," he concludes.

### ◆ Conclusion

Uncle Sam's multitude of "public servants" and other hangers-on are clearly "eating out the substance" of our productive private economy. What is troubling is the public's passive response to the rise of the bureaucracy and special interests.

## The Federal Octopus

Government's take—whether in the form of bureaucratic compliance or influencing the process is now accepted as an unavoidable cost of doing business. It is reminiscent of the days when the mob ran the cities in the 1920s and the 1930s and demanded ten percent off the top from stores and businesses. The only difference between the mob and government is that the mob let you run the business your way. And the mob only demands ten percent.

Calvin Coolidge once captured the essence of politics when he observed in his autobiography that "nine-tenths of those who come to Washington want something they ought not to have." The primary reason that our government doesn't work anymore is that nine-tenths of the people who come to Washington now *get* what they ought not to have.

Their gain has been America's loss.

# CONCLUSION

# Taking Back Washington

> *Thank God we don't get all the government we pay for.*
> —Will Rogers

A *Fortune* magazine cover story ominously warns in bold black letters: "The Budget is Out of Control!" But the data on the article is not 1995; it's 1950. Back then, the budget had grown "out of control" because the federal government would spend a little over $200 billion a year in 1950 (in today's dollars).

What, then, is one to make of our current federal budget? This year Congress will for the first time ever surpass the one-and-a-half trillion dollar spending mark—an inglorious achievement. Worse, if we remain on the course we're on, before the turn of the century the budget will reach two trillion dollars. Between 1995 and 2000 the federal government will spend $8.5 trillion—adjusted for inflation, *that's twice the cost of winning World War I and World War II combined.* These are numbers that make our heads spin.

In the rest of America a wondrous productivity revolution is transforming American industries. American firms and workers in industry after industry are getting ever more efficient, producing more and more goods and services at lower and lower costs. They are cutting the fat, innovating, merging, working harder and smarter. In global markets Americans are competing and winning—no thanks to the shackles of taxation and regulation that government chains around their ankles.

Only Washington seems impervious to this productivity revolution. Congress provides a product that Americans view as increasingly inferior while charging an ever inflated price tag. Indeed, in many areas of government—our education and mail delivery systems, for example—a strong case could be made that productivity has been negative in recent decades. Only in the institution of government is mediocrity rewarded with larger budgets. **This is precisely why government has become America's number one growth industry.** No matter how poor its performance, it gets larger and larger.

Today Washington undertakes thousands of activities that it was never meant to do. During the New Deal and then the Great Society years, hundreds and hundreds of new, well-intended programs were invented, each with bold missions: to rebuild our cities, improve our education system, fight a war on poverty, house the poor, subsidize struggling farmers, put a man on the moon.

There was nothing government couldn't do. And there were unlimited budgets for doing it. Meanwhile, the long-standing idea that the federal government had only a few "enumerated powers" conferred to it by the Constitution—an idea strictly adhered to for nearly the first 150 years of the nation—was discarded as a bothersome anachronism. And once the dam was broken, a flood of federal spending ensued. Today, it would be difficult to identify a single activity, regulation, or spending program that Congress or the Courts would consider prohibited by the Constitution.

The legacy of this can-do era of government is a runaway budget, a $4 trillion debt, and an almost universal consensus among the voters that government is a failure. As one liberal political columnist recently lamented, "Something ugly has happened in America, voters have come to loathe their own government." And for good reason.

We need a major correction. The genie needs to somehow be stuffed back into the bottle. The process for doing so isn't going to be easy, and it isn't going to be much fun. The politics of giving is a lot more popular than the politics of self-responsibility.

## Taking Back Washington

As a start, here are some specific reforms that need to be implemented as soon as possible:

1) Enact a Balanced Budget Amendment/Spending Limit Amendment;

2) Abolish entire agencies of government, including the Departments of Energy, Education, Commerce, Labor, Agriculture, and Housing and Urban Development;

3) Really end welfare as we know it;

4) Replace the progressive income tax with a flat tax or national sales tax;

5) Impose term limits and return to a true citizen legislature; and

6) Enforce private property rights against intrusive regulation.

It has taken some sixty years for government to "get out of control." Now it is time for Americans to take back their government. What is at stake is the survival of the American idea of freedom, free enterprise, and self-government.

## About the Author

Stephen Moore is the Director of Fiscal Policy Studies at the Cato Institute. A former Grover M. Hermann fellow in budgetary affairs at the Heritage Foundation, he is the author of two previous books, *Slashing the Deficit: A Blueprint for a Balanced Budget by 1993* and *Privatization: A Strategy for Taming the Federal Budget* (with Stuart Butler). Moore is a contributing editor at the *National Review*, and his articles frequently appear in the *Wall Street Journal*, *Reader's Digest*, and *Human Events*.

Moore holds a B.A. in economics from the University of Illinois, and did his graduate work in economics at George Mason University. In 1987 he served as the research coordinator for President Reagan's National Commission on Privatization. In 1988 he served as a special consultant to the National Economic Commission, which was appointed to provide a blueprint for reducing the deficit. Most recently, he spent ten months as a visiting fellow at the Joint Economic Committee.

## About the Institute for Policy Innovation

The Institute for Policy Innovation (IPI) is a non-profit, non-partisan educational organization founded in 1987. IPI's purposes are to conduct research, aid development, and widely promote innovative and non-partisan solutions to today's public policy problems. IPI is a public foundation, and is supported wholly by contributions from individuals, businesses, and other non-profit foundations. IPI neither solicits nor accepts contributions from any government agency.

IPI's focus is on developing new approaches to governing that harness the strengths of individual choice, limited government, and free markets. IPI emphasizes getting its studies into the hands of the press and policy makers so that the ideas they contain can be applied to the challenges facing us today.

## IPI Publications

The Institute for Policy Innovation publishes a variety of public policy works throughout the year. Interested parties may receive some or all of these publications free of charge, upon request:

> *IPI Insights* is a colorful, bimonthly newsletter that contains a variety of short articles on policy topics in a popular format.
>
> **TaxAction Analysis' Economic Scorecard** is a quarterly review of the nation's economic performance, with particular emphasis on administration policy, looking especially for long-term trends.
>
> **Policy Reports** are longer, 16-60 page studies on a variety of policy topics, complete with charts, tables, graphs and endnotes.
>
> **Issue Briefs** are shorter, 4-16 page studies on a variety of policy topics, complete with charts, tables, graphs and endnotes.

### How You Can Contact the Institute for Policy Innovation

The Institute for Policy Innovation invites your comments, questions, and support. You can reach IPI in several ways, either by phone, fax, mail, email, or through our Internet Home Page.

IPI's mailing address is:
250 South Stemmons Frwy., Suite 306
Lewisville, TX 75067
(214) 219-0811 [voice]
(214) 219-2625 [fax]

IPI's email addresses are:
ipi@i-link.net
71530,3677 (CompuServe)

IPI also maintains a home page on the World Wide Web, part of the Internet. Through IPI's home page you may view, print or download any of IPI's publications in Adobe™ Acrobat™ format. You will find IPI's home page at:

http://www.metronet.com/ipi/index.html